A CAJUN FAMILY COOKBOOK

by John Gravois

Savory House Press

THE AUTHOR

Like everyone else who grew up in South Louisiana, John Gravois was raised on some of the world's greatest comfort foods. His mother, Joy, was a masterly host and cook, celebrated for her gumbos and jambalayas. As Gravois prepared to leave Houma, deep in the bayou country south of New Orleans, to go off to the University of Missouri, his mother began to write down her precious recipes — rarely shared and closely guarded — so that he would have a taste of home with him wherever his career in journalism should take him. Gravois began that career at his hometown *Houma Courier* in the 1970s. After college, he covered politics for *The Houston Post* in Austin and Washington and later became an editor at the *Fort Worth Star-Telegram,* where he's been since 1995. Building on the legacy of recipes from his mother, he has accumulated recipes from extended family and in-laws for a collection that forms the heart of this cookbook.

Cover photos by Ralph Lauer
Book & cover design by Jared Stone
Edited by Amy Culbertson

Bulk sales of books from the Great Texas Line are available at special discounts for fund raising, promotions and premiums.

Savory House Press
Post Office Box 11105
Fort Worth, Texas 76110
1-800-73TEXAS / FAX 817-926-0420

E-mail: greattexas@hotmail.com

Visit our Web site to see the entire line of Texas books:
www.savoryhousepress.com

INTRODUCTION:
The joy of cooking Cajun

IT'S MORE THAN THE FOOD. It's more than the music — more
than Mardi Gras, mudbugs and Who Dat Nation. It's the eternal
embrace of *joie de vivre,* the joy of living, that makes my Cajun
homeland of South Louisiana a paradise, albeit a steamy one.
From the bayous of Terrebonne and Lafourche parishes to the
prairies of rice country in Acadia Parish to the amazing mix of
cultures in the neighborhoods of greater New Orleans, South
Louisiana is a lush, semi-tropical region with a history as rich
as its food. It's a melting pot of influences from the people from
all corners of the world who settled there. It's a place where,
to this day, many still get a lot of ingredients the old-fashioned
way — from the bounty of nature. They fish, they hunt and they
grow their own vegetables. And if they don't, they have a friend
or relative or neighbor who does, and they swap and share, as is
the Cajun way. A good mechanic who doesn't mind taking a look
under the hood of a neighbor's car might get a sack of oysters or a
basket of tomatoes in return.

We love to celebrate and throw parades and festivals year-
round. You think department stores overdo the holidays? Check
out the front porches of some Cajun homes. Around Halloween,
when the temperatures start dipping and football is in peak
season, folks decorate with wreaths and flags in LSU purple
and gold and New Orleans Saints black and gold. The holiday
celebrations run unabated through the Christmas and New Year's
season, which, in Catholic tradition, stretches through Jan. 6,
King's Day, the Epiphany. Then Mardi Gras kicks off and carries
you through Ash Wednesday, which begins the Lenten season,
when you throw crawfish boils and fish fries until Easter. Between

then and the next football season in the fall, we hold festivals in honor of everything from possum to Ponchatoula strawberries. In fact, the good times roll in Cajun country even when times are tough. You've heard of hurricane parties? Well, they're not named for the potent fruity drink that tourists sip when walking through the French Quarter. They're the parties Cajuns throw when a storm approaches in the Gulf of Mexico. More recently, the BP oil disaster gave rise to "spill parties."

I'm fortunate to have strong family roots in the different and distinct geographical and cultural areas of South Louisiana. I grew up deep in the bayou country in Houma. My dad, Lloyd Gravois, grew up along the Mississippi River in Port Allen, just outside Baton Rouge, and once lived on Westover Plantation, where his father, Henry, worked as manager. My mom grew up in the Reed family on a rice farm near Iota — yes, there is a real town called Iota; it's just outside Crowley, which is just outside Lafayette on the Cajun prairie — and later moved to the "big town" in bayou country, Houma. My wife, Suzanne, and her family — the Roys — are "city folk," who grew up in and around New Orleans.

I learned about the joy of entertaining from my mother, Joy Gravois, who taught us all that good food, drink and conversation can make a special moment out of any occasion. She would toil for weeks to prepare for a big event like the annual office Christmas party my dad would throw, or for a weekend visit by a large group of relatives. She'd chop, slice, boil and simmer for days, stowing away the components of what would come together as a massive feast on the big day. And no matter how tired she must have been from all the preparation, she meant it when she would say the pleasure was all hers. Nothing made her happier than bringing joy to others. That was true whether she was entertaining a crowd or simply heating a pot of coffee and a slice of pie for a neighbor. If you were a guest in our home, you were pampered.

Sharing recipes on the internet might seem like second nature today, but not to most Cajuns. For one thing, everyone has some special ingredient or technique for almost every dish, and no one wants to divulge those secrets. For another, a lot of folks just don't like reducing their dishes to a specific recipe. As anyone who grew up in bayou country should be willing to admit, we're not exactly the most precise people when it comes to directions and quantities. Ask someone how to season a gumbo, and you're likely to hear about using "a little of dis" and "a lot of dat." Try to learn how long to cook a roux, and you'll probably be told to stir it until it's a certain color. I was lucky that, as I prepared to leave Houma to pursue a master's degree at the University of Missouri, my mom decided to write down a few crucial recipes for me as a matter of survival. How could I get by without knowing how to make a pot of rice? Or without knowing how to make her beloved jambalaya and red beans?

The recipes she wrote down for me were the starting point for this cookbook. Another major source of recipes and inspiration came from one of my mom's sisters, Charlotte Hewitt, and her husband, Ron. They collected recipes from my mom and my grandmother, from aunts and uncles and cousins in the Reed family tree, and compiled them into a cookbook for a family reunion. Many of those recipes are included here, as are recipes from others in the Gravois and Roy family trees. I'm grateful to all the relatives and friends who shared the recipes inside. And I'm grateful to my wife, Suzanne, my kids, Joy and Nick, and brothers, Michael and Jeffrey, for their support.

Through these recipes I hope to share the joy of cooking, entertaining and fellowship. They are dishes that are meant to be shared and enjoyed. *Laissez les bons temps rouler!*

—JOHN GRAVOIS

Contents

GUMBOS, SOUPS AND STEWS

SEAFOOD MAIN DISHES

MEAT, GAME AND FOWL MAIN DISHES

Some basics

HOW TO MAKE A ROUX

There's a reason Cajun cooks always say, "First, you start with a roux." It's the base of many dishes, the foundation for gumbos, stews and soups. It's also a challenge for some cooks to master, because it takes time and patience and a lot of stirring. If you're not careful, it's likely to burn — and if you burn it, you'll need to throw it out and start over.

There are various prepared roux mixes on the market, and I confess to using them sometimes, because they're a big time-saver and most people will never be able to tell. But if you really want to get into Cajun cooking, you've got to be able to make a roux from scratch.

The ingredients:

1/4 cup vegetable oil   1/4 cup flour
    (shortening, butter or bacon
    fat will work, too)

The technique: Use a cast-iron pot or skillet; any size will do, just make sure it is heavy cast iron. I find it easier to use a whisk, but many people stick with a spoon. Begin heating the oil in the pan over medium heat. Begin sprinkling in the flour, stirring all the while; add the flour gradually, a little every 15 seconds or so. Keep stirring after all the flour has been added. You've got to stick with it, stirring almost constantly, as the fat-and-flour mixture gets darker and darker. The slow dry heat fragments the starch molecules in the flour and develops a nutlike flavor that gives body to whatever dish you're building from it. After about 12 minutes of stirring, it ought to be turning into a nice rich brown. If you want it darker, you might go as long as half an hour; the darker the roux, the deeper the flavor. Personally, I get my desired results after about 15 minutes.

Some tips: This recipe should make enough roux for a gumbo or stew that'll serve 6 or so, but Cajun recipes vary widely in the amount of roux they call for; if the recipe you are making requires more roux, just use more oil and flour at the outset. The key is adding them in equal amounts.

If black specks appear in your roux, that's the telltale sign that it's burned, and you'll have to start over. Trust me, you won't enjoy a dish that begins with burned roux!

You can make roux ahead and refrigerate it, covered. Before you reheat it, pour off any excess oil from the surface of the chilled roux. Then transfer the roux to the skillet or pan in which you'll be making the dish and reheat over medium heat, stirring frequently.

HOW TO MAKE RICE

Many dishes in this cookbook call for cooked white rice. You'll find lots more ways to top a plate of steaming hot white rice than with red beans and étouffeé; my family even served rice for breakfast, topping it with fried eggs.

These are my mom's cooking directions, so they are to be strictly followed; this is one of the few Cajun recipes in which quantities and precision are important.

My mother's double-boiler method turned out perfect rice — she always used long-grain — with separate grains and surpassingly tender texture. These days, I do mine in one pot, which is quicker, more convenient and almost as good.

Double-boiler method: Fill the bottom of the double boiler a little more than halfway full with water.

Use a 2-to-1 ratio of water to rice; 1 cup of rice will serve 3 to 4 people. Add about 1 teaspoon of salt for each cup of rice.

Wash the rice, drain well, then put it in the top of the double boiler, add twice as much water as rice and the appropriate amount of salt. Cover, place double boiler over high heat and bring the water in the bottom to a boil. Then reduce the heat to low and cook the rice over the simmering water about 30 minutes. Fluff with fork before serving.

One-pot method: If you don't have a double boiler, you can use a regular pot. It's the same drill with a key difference in timing. For every cup of rice, use 2 cups of water and 1 teaspoon of salt. You also can add a pat or two of butter. Bring to a boil, lower heat so that water is just simmering, cover and cook about 14 minutes. Fluff rice with fork, re-cover and let sit 3 to 5 minutes before serving.

Rice cookers: My momma didn't use rice cookers, but a lot of very capable cooks I know do. So if you want to use one, that's fine — just follow the directions.

INGREDIENTS AND COOKING TERMS

Andouille: Cajuns pronounce it ahn-DOO-ee, and it's a dense, highly seasoned and heavily smoked link sausage made with large chunks of pork. Though you can substitute another spicy smoked pork link sausage, andouille has become fairly common in gourmet markets and larger supermarkets. If you have trouble finding it, fortunately, my favorite Cajun meat market — the Best Stop in Scott, La. — now has a web site, and you can order this and other great meats from the comfort of your keyboard at www.beststopinscott.com. It's also available online at www. cajungrocer.com or www.tonychachere.com.

Cane syrup: Made from sugar cane, it's the syrup of choice for many Cajuns, with Steen's (made in Abbeville, La.) being the most popular brand. If you didn't grow up eating it, you might find the flavor of cane syrup a little strong; Steen's also sells a blended cane syrup that's not so overpowering. And if you can't find Steen's, you might be able to find Fain's, a Texas-made product. Order Steen's online at www.steensyrup.com.

Crawfish: Live crawfish — the little crustaceans that pinch you with their claws and try to run away backwards — are seasonal, primarily available from early spring through early summer, although crawfish farms are now making them available for longer periods. Live crawfish typically come in 30- to 40-pound sacks and are used for boiling. When buying them this way, make sure they're still alive and pinching. And we always encourage folks to buy Louisiana or Texas crawfish. You can buy frozen whole crawfish at some Walmart stores and other retail grocers, but they're almost always from China, and my relatives won't think much of you for buying your crustaceans from overseas.

Frozen crawfish tails, already cleaned and cooked, can be found in many supermarkets and are very convenient to use. Simply thaw them in the refrigerator for several hours (or overnight); then rinse them and add them to your étouffée or jambalaya or gumbo. If you're a Cajun and you want all the flavor of the crawfish fat, don't rinse the tails; just put them directly into your dish. Frozen tails from Louisiana often still come in 16-ounce bags, but most frozen tails from overseas come in 12-ounce bags. You can order crawfish — live or boiled whole, or frozen pre-cooked tails — online at www.cajungrocer.com or www.lacrawfish.com.

Étouffée: Pronounced ay-too-FAY, it comes from the French word étouffer, which means to smother. It's a rich, savory stew — usually made with seafood such as crawfish or shrimp — traditionally started with a dark roux and served over rice.

Filé powder: Pronounced FEE-lay and often referred to as "gumbo filé," it's a common ingredient in gumbos. Filé is powdered sassafras leaves; it's used both for its flavor and its thickening properties. It's usually added toward the end of cooking, as too much heat can render it ropey, and a shaker of it is sometimes placed on the table along with the gumbo in case anyone wants to add more. Look for it in the spice aisle, or order it online at www.cajungrocer.com, www.zatarains.com or www.tonychachere.com.

Gumbo: It's the rich, dark, savory soup of life in bayou country, and there are many variations, using all kinds of fresh vegetables, seafood and meat and fowl both smoked and fresh. It's best cooked for hours over a low heat, allowing the ingredients to "get happy," as Emeril Lagasse likes to say. Although everyone has a favorite of his or her own — I can never decide between the chicken-and-sausage and the shrimp-and-crabmeat versions – there is one thing in common with every gumbo recipe I've seen: First, you start with a roux. It's customary to serve gumbo over a mound of hot white rice in the middle of the bowl. French bread and potato salad are common side dishes. While Cajuns love making gumbo from scratch, there are several mixes available on the market that work quite well; just follow the directions. Order them online at www.cajungrocer.com, www.zatarains.com, www.tonychachere.com or www.brucefoods.com.

Jambalaya: If gumbo is the soup of life, jambalaya is the casserole of life, at least in my family. It's basically a jazzed-up rice dressing with meat and/or seafood added. There are two basic varieties: red jambalaya, made with tomato sauce, and brown jambalaya, made with a brown gravy. Like gumbo, it's best done from scratch, but there are several mixes available at many grocery stores and on the web: www.zatarains.com, www.brucefoods.com, www.tonychachere.com or www.louisianafishfry.com.

Tasso: Pronounced TAH-so, it's salt-cured, slow-smoked, intensely seasoned pork. Though sometimes referred to as "tasso ham," it's usually made from the shoulder butt, cut into strips or chunks, instead of the leg of the pig. It can be made with other meats, too, especially turkey. It's not meant to be eaten by itself, like ham, but is used to add flavor to a wide variety of dishes. A little goes a long way. It's in all the grocery stores down in South Louisiana, and a lot of meat markets make their own, but it's hard to find elsewhere. Sometimes gourmet markets carry it. Possible substitutes include smoked ham, Canadian bacon or slab bacon, but these will not lend the same intensity of flavor to a dish as will tasso, and you may want to add black pepper and cayenne, or Cajun seasoning, to compensate. Order it online at www.beststopinscott.com, www.cajungrocer.com or www.tonychachere.com.

What to use: Unless otherwise specified, when these recipes call for butter, use unsalted butter, not salted; don't substitute margarine unless the recipe indicates you can. When sugar is called for, use white granulated sugar unless otherwise specified. When rice is called for, use long-grain white rice. When flour is called for, use all-purpose flour unless otherwise specified. When fresh parsley is called for, Italian (flat-leaf) parsley is preferred but curly parsley is acceptable. When green onions are called for, either chopped or sliced, use both green tops and white bulbs unless otherwise indicated.

Breakfast

COUCHE COUCHE

*That's pronounced coosh-coosh, and it's a true Cajun classic —
basically a variation of fried cornmeal mush cooked in a heavy iron
skillet with a firm-fitting lid and eaten for breakfast. This recipe,
from my Grandma Reed, easily dates back more than a century.*
Yield: 4–6 servings

1 1/2 cups white cornmeal
1/2 cup flour
2 teaspoons salt
1 1/2 cups very hot water

2 eggs
2 teaspoons baking powder
2 tablespoons oil

In a large mixing bowl, sift together cornmeal, flour and salt. Stir
in hot water to make a light batter. Break eggs into the batter and
beat well. Stir in baking powder.

Heat the oil in a heavy 10 1/2-inch lidded cast-iron skillet on
a high burner. When the skillet is very hot, pour in the batter,
lower the heat to medium-high and cover tightly. Cook 5 minutes
without stirring, until a crust forms at the bottom of the skillet.
Reduce heat to medium-low, uncover, stir and scrape the pan with
a spatula to break up the crust, and replace cover. Cook about 15
minutes more, stirring occasionally with the spatula, scraping the
bottom of the skillet and breaking up large lumps; lower heat if
the couche couche seems in danger of burning. When ready to eat,
it should be golden-brown and resemble crumbled cornbread.

Serve in bowls with milk or cream and sugar.

CAJUN SKILLET BREAKFAST

My mother, Joy, used to whip this up when we had a crowd to feed.
As a change of pace, she'd make this for dinner. It's an easy recipe to
double. You can substitute crumbled breakfast sausage for the ham.
Yield: 4–6 servings

2 large potatoes, diced or
    sliced
1/2 cup chopped onion
1/2 cup chopped green bell
    pepper
1 stick (1/2 cup) butter or
    margarine

1 cup diced ham or crumbled
    breakfast sausage
6 eggs
1/4 cup milk
Salt, pepper and Cajun
    seasoning to taste
1 cup shredded Cheddar cheese
1/2 cup chopped green onions

While dicing or slicing the potatoes (my mom would dice them for
breakfast but would slice them like fries for the dinner version of
the dish) and chopping the onion and pepper, melt the butter over
medium heat in a skillet.

Raise the heat to medium-high; add the potatoes and cook
for 5 minutes without stirring to develop a slight crust. Add the
chopped onion and green bell pepper; reduce heat to medium and
sauté, shaking pan and stirring frequently, until the onion and
pepper are wilted and the potatoes are lightly browned. Add the
ham (or sausage), stir to mix and cook just to heat through.

While ham is heating, in a medium bowl, beat the eggs with
the milk as you would for scrambling, then pour the mixture over
the ingredients in the skillet. Stir gently to be sure ingredients are
mixed, but don't overdo it. Add salt, pepper and Cajun seasoning
to taste and cook, stirring gently, until eggs are just firm.

Sprinkle shredded cheese and green onions over the dish and
serve from the skillet.

GRITS AND SAUSAGE CASSEROLE

This recipe is from my Aunt Bit Reed in Iota, La., who has spent a lifetime feeding hungry family and friends at home on the farm, at family gatherings and football games. This is great for breakfast or brunch or for tailgating before early football games.
Yield: 4–6 servings

1 cup quick-cooking grits
1 pound breakfast sausage
1 small onion, chopped

1/3 cup chopped green bell pepper
1 1/2 cups shredded sharp Cheddar cheese, divided

Cook grits according to package directions. Lightly grease a 12-inch casserole dish and preheat oven to 350°.

In a large skillet over medium heat, crumble sausage. Add onion and green bell pepper. Cook over medium heat, stirring occasionally, until meat is browned and vegetables are tender. Drain and discard drippings.

Stir grits and 1 cup of shredded cheese into meat mixture. Spoon into prepared casserole dish. Bake at 350° for 15 minutes.

Remove casserole from oven; sprinkle remaining 1/2 cup of cheese over top; return to oven and bake for an additional 5 minutes.

FRENCH TOAST

It seems like we had this once a week growing up. That's probably about how often we'd have some stale bread in the house. You can make this with packaged white bread or sliced French bread, but in both cases stale bread is best.

You can serve this French toast with or without syrup. Cane syrup is the syrup of choice for many Cajuns (see "Ingredients and cooking terms," page 12).

Yield: 4 servings

4 eggs	1/2 stick butter or margarine
2 tablespoons milk	Powdered sugar or cinnamon,
8 slices bread	for sprinkling, optional

In a wide, shallow dish, beat eggs with milk. Soak bread in mixture to coat completely.

Meanwhile, melt butter in a skillet over medium-high heat.

Cook bread in butter until browned on each side. Sprinkle with powdered sugar or cinnamon if you like, or pass the syrup.

NOVA SCOTIA OATCAKES

My Aunt Charlotte provided this tasty, healthy twist on pancakes. Nova Scotia is important to Cajun heritage because that's one of the places our ancestors settled before arriving in South Louisiana.
Yield: 8–10 cakes

3 cups rolled oats (do not use	can be substituted)
instant oatmeal)	2 tablespoons baking soda
3 cups flour, plus more for	Pinch of salt
flouring board	1 1/2 cups margarine, softened
1 cup sugar (light-brown sugar	3/4 cup cold water

Preheat oven to 325°. In a medium bowl, mix dry ingredients. Add softened margarine and mix well with hands. Stir in cold water to make a dough.

Turn dough out onto floured board and roll out about 1/2-inch thick. Cut into 3-inch squares and transfer squares with a spatula to ungreased cookie sheets. Bake for 15 to 18 minutes, until golden brown.

Serve oatcakes hot with plenty of butter and your choice of cane syrup or honey.

Appetizers, Party and Tailgating Food

HOT CRAWFISH DIP

This recipe from Cousin Kristy Reed took first place in the seafood category of a 4-H competition. She won the first time she ever entered a cooking contest, more proof that the Reed family is blessed with an abundance of good cooks.
Yield: 12–14 servings

1 pound frozen peeled, cleaned
    crawfish tails, defrosted
    (see "Ingredients and
    cooking terms," page 12)
1/2 cup light margarine

1/2 cup chopped green onions
2 teaspoons garlic powder
1 teaspoon cayenne pepper
2 (8-oz.) packages light cream
    cheese, softened

Rinse crawfish tails and set aside to drain.

In a 2-quart saucepan over medium heat, melt margarine. Add green onions, garlic powder and cayenne pepper and sauté, stirring occasionally until onions are tender. Add crawfish, along with any liquid remaining in the package, and sauté, stirring frequently, for 5 minutes. Add cream cheese, stirring until cream cheese is thoroughly mixed with all the ingredients and heated through. If the mixture seems too thick, add a little more margarine until you get the desired dipping consistency.

Serve with crackers, chips or buttered toast.

HOT CRAB DIP

Here's a basic dip enjoyed in many Cajun households, often a day or two after a big crab boil that results in leftover crabmeat. This is one case, though, when canned crabmeat is acceptable. You can add or substitute finely chopped shrimp, too. If you're using stale bread rather than purchased seasoned bread crumbs for the crumb topping, just toss the crumbs with a little of the Cajun seasoning.
Yield: 8 servings

1 cup crabmeat, fresh or
    canned
8-oz. package cream cheese,
    softened (low-fat is
    acceptable)

1/4 cup chopped green onions
Dash of Worcestershire sauce
Cajun seasoning to taste
2 tablespoons seasoned bread
    crumbs

Preheat oven to 350°. In a medium bowl, gently blend together all the ingredients except bread crumbs. Scrape into small casserole dish, sprinkle bread crumbs over the top and bake 20 to 25 minutes, until top is browned and casserole bubbly.

COLD CRAB DIP
Yield: 6 servings

1 cup crabmeat
1 cup mayonnaise
1/2 cup grated Cheddar cheese
1 tablespoon bottled French
    dressing

1 tablespoon Worcestershire
    sauce
1/2 tablespoon horseradish,
    optional

In a medium bowl, gently fold together all the ingredients until well-mixed. Cover and chill overnight. Serve over Melba rounds or your favorite crackers; it's also good with celery.

ARTICHOKE DIP

If there's a card game, potluck dinner or family gathering, somebody is going to bring artichoke dip. Here's a version from my mother-in-law, Helen Roy. She's not a Cajun, even though she lives in Houma. She's originally from Philadelphia, and she spent much of her adult life in and around New Orleans, where the locals do not consider themselves Cajuns; they're New Orleanians. We call them Y'ats. That's because, rather than greeting each other with a "How you doing?" they'll ask, "Where y'at?"
Yield: 8 servings

14-oz. can artichoke hearts, drained and mashed or chopped
1 cup mayonnaise
2 cups sour cream
.6-oz. package dry Italian salad dressing mix
1/4 cup sliced green onions, for garnish

In a small bowl, combine all ingredients. Transfer to a serving dish and garnish with green onions.

HOT ARTICHOKE AND PARMESAN SPREAD

This comes from Cousin Kristy Reed and is a nice lower-fat twist on artichoke dip.
Yield: 6–8 servings

1 cup low-fat cottage cheese
1/2 cup grated Parmesan cheese
3 tablespoons non-fat mayonnaise
2 cloves garlic, minced
1/4 teaspoon hot sauce
14-oz. can artichoke hearts, drained and finely chopped
Vegetable oil cooking spray
Whole-wheat Melba toast rounds

Preheat oven to 350°. In large mixing bowl (use an electric mixer if you have one), blend cottage cheese, Parmesan, mayonnaise, garlic and hot sauce, mixing until smooth. Stir in artichoke hearts.

Spray a 1-quart baking dish with vegetable oil. Spoon in the mixture. Bake 20 minutes, or until thoroughly heated. Serve with Melba rounds.

LOUISIANA CHEESE AND SAUSAGE DIP

My Aunt Debbie Reed served up this recipe. It's sort of a Cajun queso.
Yield: 14–16 servings

1/4 cup butter or margarine
1 pound smoked andouille sausage, or other smoked pork sausage, diced
1 cup chopped onions
1/4 cup chopped celery
1/4 cup red or green bell pepper
2 tablespoons minced garlic
12-oz. jar jalapeños, seeded and chopped

2 pounds Velveeta cheese, diced, at room temperature
4 cups mayonnaise
Salt and pepper to taste
Louisiana pepper sauce — Crystal, Louisiana Brand, Tabasco, whichever brand you prefer — to taste
1/4 cup chopped fresh parsley

In a heavy saucepan, melt butter over medium-high heat. Add sausage, onions, celery, bell pepper and garlic. Sauté, stirring frequently, until vegetables are wilted. Add jalapeños and sauté 2 to 3 minutes. Remove from heat and allow to cool.

Transfer mixture to a mixing bowl; add Velveeta and mayonnaise and blend together until smooth. Season with salt, pepper and the pepper sauce. Sprinkle in parsley. Blend together until well mixed (can be made in advance up to this point). To serve, transfer to microwave-safe serving bowl and heat to desired serving temperature in microwave.

ANDREW'S BACON WRAPS

This recipe from my cousin's son, Andrew Reed, won the award for best overall dish at the International Rice Festival cooking contest in Crowley, La., when he was 10. Crowley bills itself as the rice capital of the world, so winning a cooking contest there is a big deal.

Tasso is slow-smoked, intensely seasoned pork (see "Ingredients and cooking terms," page 14). You can substitute smoked ham or Canadian bacon, but the flavor will be milder. To compensate, you could add more black pepper and a little cayenne.

These can be made ahead and broiled at the last minute.
Yield: 15–20 wraps

2 cups cooked rice
1/2 cup chopped tasso
1/2 cup chopped green onions
2 tablespoons chopped fresh
    parsley
Salt and pepper to taste
2 ounces cream cheese,
    at room temperature
2 tablespoons milk
1 tablespoon mayonnaise
1 teaspoon horseradish
8-oz. can sliced water
    chestnuts, drained
1/2 pound sliced bacon,
    each slice cut into thirds
    crosswise

In a large bowl, combine rice, tasso, green onions, parsley, salt and pepper and stir well.

In a separate small bowl, mix together cream cheese and milk, mashing the cream cheese into the milk as you blend. Mix in mayonnaise and horseradish, stirring well. Add this mixture to the rice mixture and stir until well blended.

Take about 1 tablespoon of rice mixture at a time and form into balls. Insert 1 slice of water chestnut into each ball; wrap ball with a piece of bacon and secure with a toothpick. Place balls on a cookie sheet or baking pan shallow enough to go into broiler.

Just before serving, preheat oven to 450° and broil for about 20 minutes, or until golden brown.

BOILED CRAWFISH

There's no better way to spend an evening in Cajun Country than having a crawfish boil with family and friends.

The best way to do it is to go to someone else's house, because of the effort and cleanup involved, and the necessity of having the right equipment — namely, a propane gas burner with a base and a 30-quart stainless-steel boiling pot with a stainless-steel basket inside.

And, of course, you've got to live in a region where you can get your hands on a 30- to 40-pound sack of live crawfish. Once, you pretty much had to live in South Louisiana or southeast Texas or the greater Houston area to be able to procure the crustaceans. But now you can find crawfish at grocery stores and seafood markets in other areas.

Even after acquiring the equipment and crawfish, it's quite a process – but the fun times you'll have pinching tails when it's all ready can make it well worth the effort!

Yield: 10–12 servings

30 to 40 pounds live crawfish (see "Ingredients and cooking terms," page 12)

1 pound cayenne pepper

4 oz Tabasco or your choice of Cajun red hot sauce

20 cloves garlic, cut in half

2 dozen lemons, sliced in half

2 pounds salt

10 (3-oz.) bags of Zatarain's or other brand of crawfish, shrimp and crab boil (can substitute 16 ounces of concentrated liquid boil)

8 pounds small red potatoes, cleaned

12 ears fresh corn, cleaned and broken in half (frozen ears can be substituted)

2 pounds small fresh mushrooms, cleaned (any variety will work)

4 pounds andouille sausage, cut into large chunks (4 pounds of smoked cocktail sausages can be substituted)

4 large yellow onions, cut in quarters

Buy your sack of live crawfish no earlier than the day before the boil. You need to keep the critters alive until you're ready to dump them into the boiling water — and that means keeping them in an ice chest or large container out of direct sunlight.

Some folks "purge" their crawfish; some don't. What that means is to soak the crawfish in the ice chest in cold fresh water for a few hours before the boil; some people add a pound of salt to aid the process, but that's optional. This process, in polite terms, allows the mud bugs to "purge" the "mud" from their systems.

While the crawfish await their fate, fill your boiling pot about two-thirds full with fresh, clean water; add the cayenne, hot sauce, garlic, lemon halves, salt and seafood boil and turn up the burner! Heating that big pot to a full boil can take quite a while — it might take an hour — and that's when the beer-drinking usually begins.

When the pot comes to a full boil, you'll have to decide whether you need to do the crawfish in one or two batches. If you do two batches, obviously you'll want to split the ingredients accordingly.

Either way, add the potatoes first and let them boil for 10 to 12 minutes by themselves, because they take the longest to cook. Then add the crawfish, corn, mushrooms and sausage. After the mixture returns to a full boil, cook for about 12 minutes, turn off the fire and then let everything soak in the spicy, steaming broth for another 10 to 12 minutes.

Remove the basket from the cooker to drain; dump the contents on a large picnic table covered with newspapers, spread them out and dig in!

Traditionally, Cajuns serve themselves with large, round trays like you see in restaurants and lounges. It's vital to have rolls of paper towels and garbage cans nearby.

How to peel crawfish: You've probably seen the racy version of this on T-shirts or plastic cups before, but here's a description that can safely be used in a family publication.

1. Hold the head in one hand and twist off the tail with the other.
2. Peel off the top few segments of the tail shell, exposing the tail meat.
3. Pinch the fan of the tail between your thumb and forefinger, twist a bit and pull the meat from the shell, either with your fingers or with your teeth.
4. If you're feeling adventurous, you can suck the flavor-packed juices from the head and claws.

BOILED SHRIMP

This is a much quicker and easier way to enjoy boiled seafood than boiling up a sack of live crawfish. And, unless you're one of the fortunate few who live close enough to the coast to buy your shrimp by the ice chest, you would typically do this in much smaller batches than crawfish. You can do it inside on the stove with a large soup pot.

The key is to use large shrimp — 16 to 20 per pound — and to take care not to overcook them, or let them sit too long before you eat them.

When possible, use wild-caught shrimp from the Gulf of Mexico; they're labeled that way at your grocery store. Fresh Gulf shrimp have a distinct sweetness that sets them apart from all others.

If you want to boil shrimp to serve chilled, perhaps with the remoulade sauce on page 28, just omit the potatoes, corn and mushrooms. Peel the drained shrimp as soon as they are cool enough to handle, store them in a sealed container and refrigerate them.
Serves 4–5

1/4 cup salt
1 large onion, quartered
4 large lemons, halved, seeded
6 tablespoons cayenne pepper
6 tablespoons Tabasco or other Cajun hot sauce
3-oz. bag Zatarain's or other brand of seafood boil (4 oz. concentrated liquid boil can be substituted)
1 pound small Yukon Gold potatoes (small red potatoes can be substituted)
4 ears of corn, cleaned and broken in half
1 pound cremini (baby Portobello) mushrooms, optional (or small button mushrooms)
5 pounds large (16–20 per pound) headless Gulf shrimp

Fill large soup pot about two-thirds full with water; add salt and bring to a boil. Add onion, lemons, cayenne, Tabasco and seafood boil, stir and let the flavors come together a couple minutes before adding the potatoes. Let potatoes boil for 12 minutes; then add corn and mushrooms and boil for another 5 minutes. Add shrimp and boil for 3 minutes, no more! Remove pot from burner and let sit for 2 more minutes, then drain contents in a large colander or sieve; serve right away to peel and eat.

SEAFOOD SAUCE

Almost any cocktail sauce, or even ketchup, will suffice for dipping boiled seafood, but here's a quick, easy sauce that my wife whips up whenever we have a crawfish boil. The recipe can be easily doubled or tripled.
Yield: 6–8 servings

1/2 cup mayonnaise or Miracle Whip salad dressing
1/4 cup ketchup
1/8 teaspoon Tabasco or other hot red sauce
1/2 teaspoon Cajun seasoning

Combine all ingredients in a bowl. Chill and serve.

REMOULADE SAUCE FOR SHRIMP

This is a sauce my mom used to pour over the peeled, boiled shrimp that she put out as a featured attraction at holiday parties and for special occasions. Back in the 1970s, I recall, my dad would go down the bayou and get the shrimp freshly canned from the docks. Of course, you can also use this sauce for lump crabmeat, fish or lobster.
Yield: enough to coat 2 to 3 pounds of shrimp, or 12–14 servings

4 tablespoons lemon juice
4 tablespoons tarragon vinegar
4 tablespoons prepared
    mustard (yellow, Dijon or
    Creole, your preference)
4 tablespoons prepared
    horseradish
2 tablespoons ketchup,
    optional

1/2 cup minced green onions
2 teaspoons salt
2 teaspoons paprika
1/2 teaspoon black pepper
Dash of cayenne pepper
1 cup salad oil
1/2 cup finely chopped celery
2 to 3 pounds peeled, boiled
    shrimp

In a medium mixing bowl, using electric mixer, combine lemon juice, vinegar, mustard, horseradish, ketchup (if using), green onions, salt, paprika, black pepper and cayenne. Gradually add oil, blending with beater. Stir in celery and mix well.

Fold peeled, boiled shrimp into the sauce, or pour the sauce over the shrimp, to coat thoroughly. After coating shrimp, chill for 2 to 3 hours (longer wouldn't hurt) before serving. The only accessory this dish needs is toothpicks.

BARBECUE SAUCE

This is another of my mom's legendary homemade sauces. She made it primarily to go with whatever meat and sausage my dad grilled up. But this sauce is liquid goodness, and we'd serve it up at lunch the next day on nothing but a slice of French bread to sop it up. It's a good dish to double for a crowd – and to be sure you've got some left over. Like many Cajun dishes, it's often better a day or two after it's made.

Yield: 6 servings

1 stick (1/2 cup) butter
1 small onion, chopped fine
8-oz. can tomato sauce
6 tablespoons brown sugar
2 tablespoons freshly
    squeezed lemon juice

2 tablespoons Worcestershire
    sauce
2 tablespoons steak sauce (A1
    or something similar is best)
1 teaspoon salt
1 teaspoon hot-pepper sauce

In small saucepan, heat butter over medium heat, stirring occasionally, until light amber in color. Add onion and sauté 2 to 3 minutes, stirring occasionally. Add tomato sauce, brown sugar, lemon juice, Worcestershire sauce, steak sauce, salt and hot sauce. Bring to a boil, stirring constantly. Cover and simmer over low heat for 10 minutes.

Gumbos, Soups and Stews

CHICKEN AND SAUSAGE GUMBO

If you give a Cajun a roux, he'll want to make a gumbo — a rich blend of meats, seafood and vegetables swimming in savory broth. Don't hesitate to add your own touches to this basic recipe: Experiment with different meats and sausages, try wild game, use sliced okra if you like. For seafood gumbo, use shrimp and lump crabmeat instead of chicken and sausage.

I hope my relatives forgive me, but I confess that using a packaged dry gumbo or roux mix is a big time-saver. It's healthier, too, because it reduces the fat.

Yield: 8–10 servings

2 pounds andouille or other smoked sausage, sliced into rounds	2 large onions, chopped
	6 ribs celery, chopped
	6 cloves garlic, minced
2 pounds boneless chicken thighs	4 quarts chicken stock or broth
Salt and pepper to taste	2 bay leaves
Vegetable oil	1 tablespoon Cajun seasoning
1 cup flour	1 bunch green onions, chopped

In a large, heavy lidded pot over medium-high heat, cook and stir the sausage until it begins to render some of its fat. Season the chicken thighs with salt and pepper and add them to the skillet. Cook, turning the chicken and stirring the sausage occasionally, until both are well browned. Remove chicken and sausage and set aside to drain on paper towels.

Make the roux (see "How to make a roux," page 9): Measure the fat in the skillet and add enough vegetable oil to total 1 cup. Return skillet to the burner over medium heat. Gradually sprinkle in the flour and cook, stirring constantly, until the roux is at least medium brown. Add the onions, celery and garlic and cook, stirring constantly, for about 4 minutes.

Add the stock, bay leaves, Cajun seasonings and salt and pepper to taste, then the sausage and chicken. Raise heat and bring to a boil, then reduce heat to low and cook, covered, for at least 2 hours.

About 15 minutes before serving, add green onions. Remove bay leaves before serving in soup bowls over rice.

ERNA'S OYSTER GUMBO

The gumbo filé (FEE-lay) called for in this recipe is a thickening and flavoring agent made from sassafras leaves (see "Ingredients and cooking terms," page 13). Look for it in the spice aisle.

I pestered my brother-in-law, Dennis Knight, in Houma to share his mother's oyster gumbo recipe for a long time before he relented. Dennis does everything with gusto; he loves life and lives it to the fullest more than anyone I have ever known. So I wasn't surprised when he made this into a recipe and cooking lesson all-in-one. First, Dennis suggests you have a cold beer before you proceed, unless it's before noon, in which case you should have a Bloody Mary.
Yield: 6–8 servings

1/2 gallon shucked oysters with their liquid	2 tablespoons gumbo filé, divided
1 large yellow onion	Salt and pepper to taste
2 sticks celery	1 stick (1/2 cup) butter
1/2 green bell pepper	Cajun seasoning blend to taste
1 clove garlic	2 heaping tablespoons parsley flakes
1/2 cup peanut oil	2 tablespoons white vinegar
1/2 cup flour	

Place a colander in a large bowl so you can save the oysters' liquid. Pour oysters into colander and let drain while you begin preparing the gumbo.

Chop onion, celery and bell pepper, mix together in a bowl and set aside. Chop garlic and place aside from the other veggies.

In a large skillet over medium heat, heat oil hot enough that when a small pinch of flour is added, it sizzles. Add flour and stir constantly until flour is lightly browned (this is a light roux). Immediately stir in the onion, celery and green bell pepper mixture; this will cool the roux and keep it from over-browning.

Stirring constantly to keep roux and veggie mixture from burning, cook until onions are transparent. IF YOU BURN THIS MIXTURE, THROW IT AWAY AND START OVER.

Now, if everything is fine, this is a good time to transfer the roux and veggie mixture to a larger pot (make sure it has a tight-fitting lid) in which you will assemble the gumbo. (You'll need the skillet again later, though). First, stir in the reserved oyster liquid. Then stir in the garlic and 1 tablespoon of the filé. Now gradually add water to the mixture until it is the consistency of a thin soup. Bring this to a boil and then reduce heat to a simmer. Salt lightly and add pepper to taste. Do not overseason at this point, because the oysters will bring in strong seasoning when added. Let this simmer, covered, while you cook the oysters.

In the large skillet you just emptied, melt butter over medium-high heat and add drained oysters. Sprinkle Cajun seasoning liberally over the oysters and stir continually. The oysters will give up more liquid, and the mixture will begin to boil. Do not drain. Continue to cook, stirring continually, until the oysters begin frying. Do not let oysters stick or scorch. Total cooking time should be no more than 5 minutes; as soon as the oysters' edges begin to curl, remove them from the heat. (Dennis believes that anyone who ruins good oysters should have to kneel on uncooked rice as punishment).

Add the oysters to the gumbo that has been simmering; then stir in the remaining 1 tablespoon filé, parsley flakes and vinegar.

Cover pot with a tight-fitting lid and continue simmering for up to an hour, stirring occasionally. Taste and add more seasoning, if desired. Simmer longer, if you've got the time, but it's ready to be served at this point. Serve over hot white rice in a large bowl. A dash of hot sauce will add more zing. Serve with garlic bread and a good white wine.

CRAB AND CORN BISQUE

This is a great soup, and you'll be amazed at how easy it is. It's easily doubled if you're cooking for a crowd. Substitute peeled, cleaned shrimp for crab to make it a shrimp bisque. Crawfish, lobster or just about any other shellfish or seafood also works.
Yield: 6–8 servings

1 stick (1/2 cup) butter or margarine	1/4 teaspoon salt
	1/4 teaspoon pepper
1 small onion, diced	2 (14.75-oz.) cans no-salt-added cream-style corn
6 cups milk	
2 large potatoes, peeled, diced	1 pound cleaned fresh lump crabmeat
1 teaspoon Cajun seasoning	

In a large lidded saucepan or pot over medium-low heat, melt butter and sauté onion until soft. Add milk, potatoes, seasonings and corn, raise heat to high, cover and heat to boiling. Add crab, stir, reduce heat to low and cook, covered, for 30 minutes.

SEAFOOD AND MUSHROOM CHOWDER

Here's another dish from Nova Scotia. Family members raved over this chowder in Digby, N.S. The version my aunts and uncles fell in love with was made with scallops, but you can substitute shrimp, crabmeat, oysters or even cubed chicken if you prefer.

Yield: 8–10 servings

1/2 stick (1/4 cup) butter
1 medium onion, chopped
2 cloves garlic, chopped
1/2 medium green bell pepper, chopped
1 pound fresh button mushrooms, cleaned and sliced

1 pound fresh bay scallops, rinsed well
12-oz. can evaporated milk
2 1/2 cups whole milk
4 to 5 green onions, chopped
1/4 cup chopped fresh parsley
1/2 tablespoon sugar, optional
Salt and pepper to taste

In a large lidded pot over medium heat, heat the butter and sauté the onion, garlic and bell pepper, stirring frequently, until wilted. Add the sliced mushrooms and scallops and cook, uncovered, stirring occasionally, over medium heat for 10 minutes. Add evaporated and whole milk, cover, bring to a simmer and simmer over low heat for another 10 minutes.

Stir in green onions, parsley, sugar (if using) and salt and pepper. Serve hot.

SHRIMP STEW

This recipe came straight from my mom – written quickly on a small piece of paper for me and my wife to enjoy, using some of the fresh Gulf shrimp we always try to take home to Texas. It's one of the many recipes that begin with, "First, you make a roux." Part of the beauty of the dish is its simplicity. Cajun cooks originally added the eggs to stretch the dish without adding more shrimp.

Yield: 5–6 servings

2/3 cup vegetable oil	1 can chicken broth, optional
2/3 cup flour	(I added this years later)
1/2 medium onion, chopped	1 pound medium Gulf shrimp,
4 cups water	peeled and cleaned
	4 boiled eggs, sliced

In a cast-iron Dutch oven or pot, heat oil over medium heat. Blend in flour, stirring constantly, and cook until you have a medium-dark roux (see "How to make a roux," page 9). Add onion, water and broth, stirring well; raise heat to medium-high and bring to a boil. Reduce to medium-low heat and simmer, covered, for 15 minutes. Add shrimp, reduce heat to low and simmer, covered, for 30 minutes. Gently stir in sliced boiled eggs and serve.

COURT BOUILLON

Here's a basic fish and seafood stew that has been cooked and enjoyed in Cajun and French kitchens everywhere for decades. Cajuns pronounce it COO-be-yon. Any kind of firm-fleshed white fish will work here; my family typically uses red snapper or catfish or whatever my in-laws catch. Don't use an oily fish such as salmon or tuna. Add other seafood if you wish.
Yield: 8–10 servings

1 cup vegetable oil	3 teaspoons salt
1 cup flour	2 cups water
1 large onion, diced	1 pound peeled, cleaned
8-oz. can tomato sauce	shrimp
16-oz. can whole peeled	1 pound fish fillets
tomatoes	6 green onions, chopped finely
3 teaspoons black pepper	2 cloves garlic, minced
3 teaspoons red pepper	

In a cast-iron Dutch oven or pot, heat oil over medium-low heat and blend in flour. Cook, stirring constantly, until roux is dark brown.

Add the onion, tomato sauce, tomatoes from can, seasonings and water. Raise heat to medium-high and cook, stirring occasionally, until mixture comes to a boil. Lower heat, cover and simmer over low heat, for 1 1/2 hours, stirring occasionally.

Add the shrimp, fish, green onions and garlic and simmer, covered, for 20 more minutes. Serve over rice.

OYSTER STEW

The best way to almost anybody's heart – and vote – in Louisiana has always been through his stomach. That's a lesson the late U.S. Sen. Allen J. Ellender of Houma used to follow. President Richard Nixon once proclaimed Sen. Ellender America's "Chef Supreme." This was one of the recipes the senator shared with constituents in campaign flyers in the 1960s and 1970s. My father-in-law, Lennie Roy, himself a great cook from New Orleans, kept a copy.
Yield: 4–5 servings

2 1/2 tablespoons bacon drippings or fat cut from bacon
1 large onion, chopped
2 pints shucked fresh oysters with liquid
A handful of chopped fresh parsley and chopped green onion tops to taste
3 cups milk

Heat bacon fat over low heat in 3-quart saucepan; when hot, add chopped onions. Cook onions, stirring occasionally, until clear but not browned. Add oysters with liquid, then parsley and green onion tops. Cook briefly, stirring, until oysters curl. Add hot milk, stir to blend and serve immediately.

Seafood Main Dishes

For seafood gumbos, soups and stews, see
"Gumbos, Soups and Stews," page 30.

FRIED SEAFOOD

*This basic recipe and technique can be used for shrimp, crawfish
tails, oysters, fish fillets and whatever else you pull out of the bayou
or lake. If you thought it was complicated, you'll be pleasantly
surprised — and the recipe can easily be doubled for big groups.*

*This recipe is for pan-frying, but you can use a deep-fryer. People
use many different ingredients for moistening the seafood before
breading, but my wife, Suzanne, has always used mustard.*
Yield: 4–5 servings

1 cup basic yellow prepared
   mustard
4 tablespoons hot-pepper
   sauce
2 pounds large shrimp,
   cleaned and deveined, or
   an equal amount of oysters,
crawfish tails or fish fillets
2 to 3 cups cooking oil (enough
   to be at least 1/4-inch deep
   in the pan)
3 1/2 cups yellow cornmeal or
   your choice of packaged fry
   mix

In a shallow bowl, thoroughly combine mustard and hot sauce.
Dredge each piece of seafood in the mustard mixture to coat
thoroughly and place on a platter or cookie sheet; after all are
coated, refrigerate for at least half an hour to firm up the coating.

Heat the oil in a large frying pan over high heat.
Spread cornmeal or frying mix on a large plate and dredge chilled
mustard-coated seafood in it to coat.

When the oil reaches between 360° and 375°, you're ready to start frying. (If you don't have a thermometer, drop a kernel of popcorn in the oil; the oil will be hot enough when it pops ' or dip the tip of the handle of a wooden spoon in the oil; if you get lots of rapid bubbles, it's ready.) A few at a time, slip the seafood into the hot oil and fry until golden brown, about 7 minutes for fish, 4 to 5 minutes for other seafood. Don't crowd the pan, or the heat will drop and you'll get soggy, greasy seafood. Drain the fried seafood on paper towels.

BOILED SHRIMP

See "Appetizers, Party and Tailgating Food," page 26.

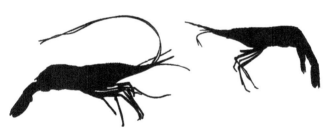

SHRIMP CREOLE

This is a classic Louisiana dish that'll serve a crowd. Cajuns love to cook for friends and family, and that's why many of our recipes make such large batches. Cooks often will tell you when a recipe is good for doubling, but this one is also fine to cut in half if you don't want so much. This dish – like many Cajun dishes – improves overnight; it's even better made the day before and reheated. It also freezes well.

The recipe is from my Aunt Nell Stephens in Natchitoches, home of legendary meat pies and of Northwestern State University, where former New Orleans Saints quarterback Bobby Hebert played college football.

Yield: 8–10 servings

1/4 cup bacon grease
1/4 cup flour
1 1/2 cups chopped onions
1 cup chopped green onions
1 cup chopped celery with leaves
1 cup chopped green bell pepper
2 cloves garlic, minced
6-oz. can tomato paste
16-oz. can chopped tomatoes
8-oz. can tomato sauce
1 cup water
5 teaspoons salt

1 tablespoon lemon juice
1 teaspoon ground black pepper
1 teaspoon sugar
1 teaspoon Worcestershire sauce
1/2 teaspoon red pepper, optional
Hot-pepper sauce to taste
2 to 3 bay leaves
4 pounds peeled, cleaned raw shrimp
1/2 cup chopped fresh parsley
3 cups hot cooked rice

In a large, heavy pot, heat bacon grease over medium-low heat. Stir in flour and cook, stirring constantly, to make a dark-brown roux. Add onions, green onions, celery, bell pepper and garlic and sauté, stirring frequently, until soft. Add tomato paste and mix well with vegetables; then stir in all other ingredients except shrimp, parsley and rice. Blend thoroughly.

Bring to a simmer, cover pot and simmer slowly for 1 hour, stirring occasionally.

Add shrimp, cover pot and cook just until shrimp turn pink. This may take from 5 to 15 minutes, depending on size, but it is important not to overcook. As soon as shrimp turn pink, remove pot from heat and let sit, covered, about 20 minutes before stirring in parsley and serving over rice.

HURRICANE BETSY SHRIMP JAMBALAYA

This recipe became family legend because it's what my Grandma Reed made the night Hurricane Betsy roared ashore in 1965, causing major damage throughout much of South Louisiana. After Betsy knocked out power to Acadia Parish, a group of my relatives ate this by candlelight as they listened to battery-powered radio to get the latest news on the storm.

Yield: 4–5 servings

1/4 cup oil	1 teaspoon salt
1 large onion, chopped	1/4 teaspoon ground red
3 ribs celery, chopped	pepper
1 large green bell pepper,	1 pound raw shrimp, peeled
chopped	and cleaned
3 cups water	Vegetable oil spray
8-oz. can tomato sauce	1 1/2 cups raw rice

Heat oil in a large skillet or pot over medium heat and sauté vegetables, stirring frequently, for 15 minutes. Do not let mixture brown.

Add water, tomato sauce, seasonings and shrimp and continue to cook over medium heat, uncovered and stirring occasionally, for 5 to 10 minutes, just until shrimp turns pink.

Meanwhile, preheat oven to 350° and coat the interior of a lidded Dutch oven or casserole dish (4 1/2-quart capacity is best) with vegetable oil spray.

Add the rice to the pot, stir everything together; then transfer to the prepared casserole dish, cover and bake at 350° for 1 hour.

EASY SHRIMP PASTA

This is another quick and easy recipe courtesy of another cousin, Connie Trahan. And it's a great way to use leftover boiled shrimp.
Yield: 6–7 servings

1 stick (1/2 cup) butter
1 1/2 onions, chopped
1 green bell pepper, chopped
1 clove garlic, chopped
1 cup half-and-half
1 tablespoon flour

8 to 10 fresh button mushrooms, sliced
1 1/2 pounds Velveeta or other processed cheese, cubed
1 pound medium boiled shrimp, peeled
1 pound pasta, any shape

In a large, heavy skillet or pot over medium heat, melt butter. When hot, add onion, bell pepper and garlic; sauté, stirring frequently, until tender. Stir in remaining ingredients except for pasta, in order listed, and cook over medium heat, stirring occasionally, until cheese is melted. Lower heat to low and simmer, covered, stirring occasionally, for 15 minutes.

Meanwhile, prepare pasta as directed, drain and combine with shrimp and cheese mixture.

EVEN EASIER SHRIMP AND TASSO PASTA

This is as simple as it gets. My wife and I picked this up at a cooking show in Houston — from some transplanted Cajuns, of course — soon after we were married. Basically, it's done in the time it takes you to boil up a pound of pasta. The key ingredient is tasso — intensely spiced and smoked pork — or beef or turkey or alligator (see "Ingredients and cooking terms," page 14). You can substitute finely diced ham or crumbled crisp bacon. It's easy to make this a healthier dish by using "light" butter and nonfat half-and-half.

Yield: 6–7 servings

1 pound rotini or pasta of your choice	1/4 pound tasso, finely diced
1 stick (1/2 cup) butter	2 cups half-and-half
1 small onion, chopped	Cajun seasoning to taste
1 pound shrimp	Hot-pepper sauce to taste, optional

Prepare pasta as directed on package. As pasta water is coming to a boil, melt butter in a skillet over medium heat, add onion and cook, stirring occasionally, until tender. Add shrimp and tasso and sauté, stirring and shaking pan, about 5 minutes, only until shrimp are pink; be careful not to overcook shrimp.

Drain pasta and toss with shrimp mixture. Add half-and-half and Cajun seasoning; you might also add a few dashes of your favorite hot-pepper sauce.

SHRIMP AND OYSTER QUICHE

Real Cajun men do not admit to cooking or eating quiche, but their wives like it, and sometimes we do, too. That's why this recipe is in this cookbook. From my nephew, Sean Stewart, in Houma, it was a prize-winner at a 4-H cooking contest.
Yield: 6 servings

2 tablespoons butter or margarine	2 eggs, beaten
	1 cup half-and-half
1 medium onion, chopped	1/4 cup freshly grated Parmesan cheese
10-oz. package frozen chopped spinach, thawed	
2 tablespoons flour	1 dozen oysters, shucked and drained
1 teaspoon salt	9-inch pie shell, baked
1/4 teaspoon pepper	

In large heavy skillet or pot, heat butter over medium-high heat. Add onion and sauté, stirring frequently, 8 to 10 minutes, until onions are wilted. Stir in spinach and sauté, stirring, for 2 minutes more. Stir in flour and seasonings, blending thoroughly. Remove from heat.

Preheat oven to 400°. In a large mixing bowl, combine eggs with half-and-half and cheese, beating well to blend. Stir in spinach mixture; blend thoroughly.

Place drained oysters in prebaked pie shell; you can leave them whole or cut them into pieces. Pour spinach mixture over oysters. Bake for 50 to 55 minutes.

CHARGRILLED OYSTERS

Variations of this dish are all the rage in New Orleans and throughout South Louisiana. But many Cajun households know a secret: It's quick and easy to do at home, and it's just as good as the restaurant variations. As long as you've got oyster shells and a charcoal grill, you're good to go. A gas grill works fine, too, but be sure to use some chips of your favorite wood to give the dish the smoky flavor that makes it so special.

It's important to try to retain as much of the oyster liquor and butter-garlic mixture as possible in the oyster shells: If you like, you can fill your serving platter with rock salt and nestle the oyster shells in the rock salt as you remove them from the grill. If you have an ovenproof serving platter, you can heat the platter with the salt in the oven before transferring the grilled oysters to the platter; the heated salt will keep the oysters hot longer (though it's not likely your guests will give them much chance to cool).

These are equally welcome as an entrée or appetizer. For an entrée, figure six oysters a person (or a full dozen for Cajuns); for an appetizer, three a person, depending, of course, on the size of the oysters. The recipe below is for a dozen but can be multiplied ad infinitum.

Yield: 1 dozen oysters; 2 entrée or 4 appetizer servings

1/4 cup olive oil
2 sticks (1 cup) butter
2 teaspoons chopped garlic
1/2 teaspoon black pepper
12 oyster shells (or as many as you have oysters)
1-pint container of large oysters (about 12), with liquor

1/4 cup each grated Parmesan and Romano cheeses (or 1/2 cup of either)
1/4 cup chopped green onions
1 tablespoon chopped fresh parsley
Hot sauce to taste

Preheat grill outside. You want the heat to be medium-high when you start cooking the oysters.

In the kitchen, in a 10-inch sauté pan over medium-low heat, melt the oil and butter with the garlic and pepper.

When coals are glowing and covered with gray ash, place oyster shells, cup side up, on the grill. Place an oyster in each and divide the oyster liquor remaining in the container among the shells. Spoon the butter and garlic mixture over the oysters, dividing it equally; then top each oyster with a sprinkling of cheese, green onion and parsley. Grill over medium-high heat until oysters have a puffed-up appearance.

With tongs, being careful not to spill any of the liquid in the shells, transfer oyster shells to a platter. Hit each oyster with a dash of hot sauce and dig in immediately.

CRAWFISH BOIL

See "Appetizers, party and tailgating food," page 24.

CRAWFISH ÉTOUFFÉE

*This is our version of a classic Cajun dish, a recipe that has been
passed around in our family for years and does well doubled.
Étouffée is traditionally started with a dark roux, but this recipe
skips the roux, which makes it relatively quick and simple; you
can have it on the table in an hour's time, start to finish. You may,
however, let your friends think you worked over a hot stove for hours.*

*If you prefer, substitute shrimp for an equally delicious shrimp
étouffée.*

Yield: 5–6 servings

1 stick (1/2 cup) margarine
1 large onion, chopped
1 medium green bell pepper,
  chopped
1 rib celery, chopped
3 cloves garlic, chopped
1 jalapeño pepper, finely
  chopped
10.75-oz. can cream of

mushroom soup
1 pound frozen peeled, cleaned
  crawfish tails, defrosted
  (see "Ingredients and
  cooking terms," page 12)
Salt and pepper to taste
Hot-pepper sauce, optional
3 green onion tops, chopped
Chopped fresh parsley to taste

In a 12-inch lidded skillet or other large pot, melt margarine over
medium heat and sauté onion, bell pepper, celery, garlic and
jalapeño until onions are light golden and translucent.

Stir in soup. Mixture will be very thick. You may have to add
water, 1/4 cup at a time, to achieve the desired consistency of a
rich gravy. Bring to a simmer, reduce heat to low and simmer,
covered, 10 to 15 minutes, stirring occasionally.

Add crawfish, cover and simmer 20 minutes more, stirring
occasionally. Add salt and pepper to taste, plus hot-pepper sauce
if you want more of a kick. Stir in onion tops and parsley and
simmer, covered, stirring occasionally, for another 10 minutes.

Serve over hot cooked rice.

CRAWFISH AU GRATIN

Here's a variation of another Cajun classic, this one from my Aunt Bit Reed, whose family knows crawfish. Years ago, it was all about rice and soybeans on the family farm near Iota. But in recent years, rice country also has become crawfish country, as farmers diversified into raising crawfish for commercial sale in the same fields in which crops are planted. The biggest side benefit was that, if it was a big year for crawfish, relatives sometimes might get a few pounds of peeled tails.

Crabmeat and shrimp also take well to the gratin treatment; you can substitute either or both for the crawfish.

Yield: 4–5 servings

1/2 stick (4 tablespoons) margarine
1 small onion, diced
2 ribs celery, chopped
1 clove garlic, minced
2 green onions, chopped
1/4 cup chopped pimiento
1 tablespoon flour
1/4 pound mild Cheddar cheese, grated, plus additional for garnish
5.33-oz. can evaporated milk
1/4 teaspoon salt
1/4 teaspoon pepper
1 pound frozen peeled, cleaned crawfish tails, defrosted (see "Ingredients and cooking terms," page 12)

In a 12-inch skillet over a medium-high burner, heat margarine and sauté onion, celery and garlic, stirring frequently, until onion becomes translucent. Add green onions and pimiento. Reduce heat to low and simmer, stirring occasionally, for 10 minutes.

Preheat oven to 375° and grease a 2-quart casserole dish.

Stir flour into vegetable mixture in skillet to blend thoroughly. Stir in Cheddar, evaporated milk, salt and pepper; cook and stir until cheese is melted. Stir in crawfish, along with any liquid in the package.

Transfer to prepared casserole dish and bake at 350° just until golden and bubbly, about 20 minutes. Sprinkle with additional cheese to garnish.

HITACHI CRAWFISH JAMBALAYA

Here's a Cajun rice cooker recipe from my cousin, Connie Trahan, and her husband Vince.
Yield: 6 servings

2 1/2 cups raw rice
10.5-oz. can beef bouillon
1 medium onion, chopped
1 medium green bell pepper, chopped
1 fresh jalapeño pepper, chopped
4-oz. can mushrooms

1 pound frozen peeled, cleaned crawfish tails, defrosted (see "Ingredients and cooking terms," page 12)
1 stick (1/2 cup) margarine, melted
8-oz. can tomato sauce
Salt and pepper to taste

Wash rice, drain well and put into rice cooker. Add bouillon, onion, bell pepper and jalapeño.

Drain liquid from mushrooms, chop and add to mixture.

Chop crawfish tails in halves and add along with margarine and tomato sauce. Stir well. Add salt and pepper to taste. DO NOT ADD WATER.

Cover and set rice cooker on cook cycle. At end of cooking cycle, set cooker on warm for 30 minutes before serving.

CRAWFISH FETTUCCINE

This is another tasty dish from the home of my cousin, Bradley Reed, who once was a standout football player for the Iota Bulldogs. Yes, it's a lot of butter. Use "light" butter if you prefer.
Yield: 6–8 servings

3 sticks (1 1/2 cups) butter
3 medium onions, chopped
2 stalks celery, finely chopped
2 bell peppers, chopped (green is traditional, but any color will do)
1/2 cup flour
1 quart half-and-half
1 pound Velveeta or other processed cheese spread, cut into 1/2-inch cubes
3 cloves garlic, chopped
4 tablespoons chopped fresh parsley
2 tablespoons minced jalapeño peppers
Salt and pepper to taste
3 pounds frozen cooked, cleaned crawfish tails, defrosted (see "Ingredients and cooking terms," page 12)
1 pound fettuccine pasta
1/4 cup grated Parmesan cheese

In a large lidded skillet over medium-high heat, melt butter. When it is hot, add onions, celery and bell pepper and cook, stirring frequently, until tender. Stir in flour until thoroughly blended, reduce heat to low, cover and cook 20 more minutes, stirring often.

Add half-and-half, cheese, garlic, parsley and jalapeños. Stir to blend thoroughly. Stir in salt and pepper to taste. Cover and cook over low heat for 20 minutes, stirring occasionally; then stir in crawfish along with any liquid in the package.

Meanwhile, cook fettuccine as directed, preheat oven to 350° and butter a large casserole dish.

When pasta is al dente, drain and transfer to the prepared casserole dish. Add the crawfish-cheese mixture, stirring and tossing to coat. Sprinkle with Parmesan. Bake at 350° for 15 minutes or until bubbly.

CRAWFISH AND CHEESE RICE QUICHE

Yeah, I know, another quiche recipe. But this one is good too. It's from a cousin, Camille Richard, and it was a prize-winner in the Rice Festival cooking contest.

Yield: 6 servings

1 tablespoon vegetable oil
1/2 cup chopped onion
2 cups cooked rice
1 medium tomato, chopped, drained, divided
1/4 teaspoon salt
1/4 teaspoon pepper
1 cup cooked spinach (frozen is fine)
1/2 pound frozen peeled, cooked crawfish tails, defrosted (see "Ingredients and cooking terms," page 12)
1/2 cup shredded Swiss cheese
1/2 cup shredded mozzarella
5 eggs
2/3 cup half-and-half
1/2 teaspoon seasoned salt
1/4 teaspoon ground nutmeg
1/4 teaspoon ground red pepper
1/4 cup grated Parmesan cheese

Preheat oven to 350° and grease an 8-inch casserole dish. In large skillet over medium burner, heat oil and sauté onion, stirring frequently, until translucent. Stir in rice, all but 1/4 cup of the tomato and the salt and pepper; cook, stirring frequently, an additional 2 to 3 minutes.

Transfer rice mixture to prepared baking dish. Spread spinach over rice mixture; top with crawfish, then with Swiss and mozzarella cheeses.

In a medium bowl, beat eggs. Stir in half-and-half, seasoned salt, nutmeg and red pepper until thoroughly blended; pour over cheese layer in baking dish. Sprinkle reserved 1/4 cup tomato on top, then Parmesan cheese.

Bake at 350° for 35 to 40 minutes, or until firm and golden brown. Garnish as desired; you can add some zip by sprinkling with Cajun seasoning before serving.

CRABMEAT, RICE AND EGGPLANT CASSEROLE

As with quiche, not everyone embraces eggplant dishes, but in my youth it was a rare summer when someone wasn't sharing a crop of homegrown eggplants that just wouldn't quit. Here's a tasty version from my Aunt Bit.

You can use leftover cooked eggplant or cook the eggplant before you start the recipe: Peel the eggplant, slice it into rounds about an inch thick, liberally salt both sides of the rounds and let them drain in a colander or spread out on paper towels for about an hour. Rinse the slices and pat dry; then coat sparingly with vegetable or olive oil and either grill the slices or roast them on a baking sheet in a 475° oven until soft.

Yield: 4–5 servings

1/2 stick (1/4 cup) butter
1 cup chopped green onions
1/2 cup chopped celery
1/2 cup chopped green bell pepper
1/4 cup chopped red bell pepper
3 cups cubed cooked eggplant
1 1/2 cups cooked rice
1 1/2 cups fresh crabmeat
1/2 pound fresh button mushrooms, sliced thinly (an 8-oz. can of mushrooms may be substituted as a last resort)
1 teaspoon salt
1/2 teaspoon black pepper
1/2 teaspoon seasoned salt
Chopped fresh parsley, optional

Preheat oven to 350°. Grease a 13-by-9-by-2-inch casserole dish.

In a large heavy skillet or pot over a medium-high burner, heat butter. When hot, sauté green onions, celery and bell peppers until onions become translucent. Add eggplant, rice, crabmeat, mushrooms, salt, pepper and seasoned salt.

Pour into prepared casserole dish. Bake at 350° until top is golden and bubbly, about 20 minutes. To serve, sprinkle top with parsley, if desired.

PECAN-CRUSTED FISH

Here is a terrific variation on fried fish whose ease and simplicity will amaze you. You can oven-fry it as directed or pan-fry it in a little oil.
Yield: 5–6 servings

2 pounds fish fillets (any white-fleshed, non-oily fish)	1/2 stick (4 tablespoons) butter, melted
2 cups buttermilk	1 cup corn flour or fish fry mix
	2 cups finely chopped pecans

In a medium bowl, submerge the fillets in the buttermilk, cover, refrigerate and let them soak for at least an hour.

When ready to cook, coat the bottom of a shallow baking pan with the melted butter and preheat oven to 425°.

In a zip-lock plastic bag, mix together the corn flour or fry mix and the chopped pecans. Add fillets, one or two at a time, seal and shake gently until fish are evenly coated with dry mixture.

Place the fillets on the prepared baking pan in a single layer. Place in preheated oven and bake at 425° for 12 to 20 minutes, depending on the size of the fillets; remove them when the edges are golden-brown and the fish is just barely beginning to flake (fish will continue to cook after being removed from the oven, so do not overcook).

FISH WITH SATSUMA SALSA OVER RICE

There are more ways to prepare fish in a Cajun kitchen than fried, broiled or blackened. This one's a favorite of my wife, Suzanne, because it's healthy and tasty. If you cook it in South Louisiana, which boasts some wonderful citrus orchards, you can make it with fresh, locally grown ingredients. My personal favorite is the satsuma, a seedless, easily peeled variety of mandarin orange that's a cousin of the imported clementines that start showing up in grocery stores before Christmas (the satsuma grows larger down the bayou than the clementine, though). You can pick your own at lots of places in Louisiana, typically from around Thanksgiving through early January. If you can't find satsumas, use clementines or mandarin oranges, seeded. You'll need 10 or 12 of them.

This works with most types of fish — redfish, snapper, trout, catfish, whatever you've got.

Yield: 6 servings

Salsa:
4 satsumas, peeled and diced, with juice (about 1 cup)
1 cup chopped tomatoes
1/2 cup diced red onion
1/4 cup finely chopped green onions

1/4 cup diced celery
1/4 cup chopped fresh cilantro
2 tablespoons extra-virgin olive oil
2 tablespoons fresh lime juice

Rice:
1 cup uncooked rice

2 cups water

Fish:
6 to 8 pieces of filleted fish
Salt and pepper, or your choice of fish seasoning, to taste
2 tablespoons olive oil

1/2 cup freshly squeezed satsuma juice (from about 6 satsumas)

Salsa: Gently mix all ingredients together in a bowl. If making in advance, cover and refrigerate; allow to come to room temperature before serving.

Rice: Cook rice with water according to directions on page 10; keep warm until ready to serve.

Fish: Season fish with salt and pepper or other fish seasoning. Heat oil in a large nonstick pan over medium-high heat. Add fish and cook on both sides until slightly brown. Remove fish from pan and keep warm on a platter, tented with foil.

Add satsuma juice to pan; raise heat to bring juice to a boil, stirring often. When juice comes to a boil, reduce heat and simmer sauce about 2 minutes, stirring often, until reduced and slightly thickened.

To serve: Divide rice among 6 plates, top with fish fillets and drizzle pan sauce over the fish. Spoon salsa over fish and serve.

LENNIE'S FISH CAKES

Some of the best Cajun cooking involves leftovers. Dishes like gumbo, jambalaya and red beans are famous examples of foods that taste even better the second time you serve them. My father-in-law, Lennie Roy, an industrious man who hates to see anything go to waste, is a master at taking chunks of leftover fish that have been broiled or steamed or grilled and using them to make fabulous fish cakes a day or two later. My wife loves them for breakfast the morning after a family fish fry.
Yield: 4 to 6 cakes

1 medium baked or boiled potato, peeled	Salt and pepper to taste
1 to 1 1/2 cups of cooked fish, broken into small chunks	1 egg, beaten
1/2 cup finely chopped onion	1/2 cup Italian-seasoned bread crumbs
	1/4 cup vegetable oil

Cut cooked potato into chunks, place in a large bowl and mash well with a sturdy fork or potato masher. Add fish, onion, salt and pepper and mix well. Add egg and mix thoroughly.

Spread bread crumbs in a shallow plate. Form fish mixture into patties and dredge in bread crumbs to coat, patting lightly to help the crumbs adhere.

Heat oil in a large skillet over medium heat. When oil is hot, add the patties in one layer; do not crowd patties (cook in two batches if necessary). Fry about 4 minutes on each side, until nicely browned. Turn them only once.

Meat, Game and Fowl Main Dishes

SAUSAGE JAMBALAYA

This is a dish passed on to me in a cherished handwritten recipe from my mom. I've cooked it as often as any dish she ever taught me. Every recipe she passed along is a treasure, but none is more special than this one.

This dish is especially good for entertaining because it's easily doubled. We Cajuns prefer pork or pork-and-beef sausage to all beef because that's the way we roll.

Yield: 6–7 servings

2 tablespoons vegetable oil
1 pound smoked link sausage,
   sliced into 1/4-inch rounds
1 large onion, chopped
1 large green bell pepper,
   chopped
2 ribs celery, chopped
4 green onions, chopped
2 cups water
2 (8-oz.) cans tomato sauce
Salt to taste
2 cups raw rice
1 teaspoon chopped fresh
   parsley, or to taste, optional

Preheat oven to 375°. Rub the cooking surface of a large lidded Dutch oven or cast-iron pot with oil and heat over medium-high heat. Add sausage and sauté until browned, turning occasionally. Drain sausage on paper towels. You should have about 5 tablespoons of drippings in the pot; pour off any excess.

Return pan to medium-high burner; add onion, bell pepper, celery and green onions; sauté, stirring frequently, until tender. Add water, tomato sauce and salt and bring to a boil. Stir in cooked sausage, raw rice and parsley.

Cover pot, transfer to oven and bake at 375° for 30 minutes; then uncover and stir gently to make sure everything is well mixed; add a little water if the mixture seems to be too dry. Replace lid, lower heat to 350° and bake for another 45 minutes, checking after about 30 minutes to see if you need to add water. When rice is tender, fluff the dish with a fork, cover and let stand 10 to 15 minutes before serving with hot French bread.

RED BEANS AND RICE WITH SAUSAGE

Here's another of my mom's classic dishes. This is one of the first recipes she taught me before I left home to go off to college. It's a great dish, period, but it's extra-good for anybody who wants to cook up some terrific comfort food inexpensively and in large batches. This recipe easily doubles and is perfect for parties, tailgating and any large gathering. Serve over white rice, with some fresh French bread. Be prepared: Beans need to soak overnight before cooking. If you have a busy schedule, this dish is one that can cook all day in a slow cooker. One more tip: My mother always sprinkled 1/4 teaspoon ground ginger into the beans before soaking them overnight, to mitigate any digestive aftereffects they might have.

Yield: 8–10 servings

1 pound dried red kidney beans

1 pound andouille sausage (see "Ingredients and cooking terms," page 11; any smoked pork or beef link sausage can be substituted)

1 large onion, chopped

2 ribs celery, chopped

1 to 2 cloves garlic, chopped

2 tablespoons chopped fresh parsley

14.5-oz. can chopped tomatoes and chiles

1 bay leaf

Salt, pepper and Cajun seasoning to taste

2 1/2 cups white rice, cooked according to instructions on page 10

The night before you want to cook the beans, put them in a large lidded Dutch oven, cover them with water and allow them to soak overnight.

When you're ready to cook the beans, pour off the water, rinse the beans and sort them to remove any shriveled ones. Return the beans to the pot, cover them with fresh water, cover the pot and begin cooking the beans slowly over low heat.

Meanwhile, heat a large skillet over medium-high heat. Slice the andouille into coins 1/4 inch thick and brown the andouille in the skillet, turning occasionally. When browned, remove the sausage to paper towels to drain, leaving drippings in the skillet.

Lower the burner to medium and cook the onion, celery, garlic and parsley in the drippings from the sausage until the onions are wilted. Transfer the vegetables to the bean pot; add the drained sausage, tomatoes, bay leaf, salt, pepper and Cajun seasoning to the beans.

Raise heat to high, cover the pot and heat to boiling, then reduce heat to low and simmer for at least 2 hours (you can also cook the beans all day over low heat in a slow cooker). Check the beans occasionally, stirring each time and adding water as needed to keep the beans covered.

Remove bay leaf before serving. Serve over fresh, hot white rice.

MOM'S MEATBALLS AND GRAVY

Fortunately, my mom wrote this one down, too. These are not meatballs for spaghetti. They are meatballs cooked in a rich, easy brown gravy that goes great over rice or mashed potatoes. You can make these meatballs with ground beef, pork or veal, or any combination thereof. My mother usually used beef and pork, and I remember her making some delicious meatballs with veal. You can easily double the recipe.

Yield: 4 servings

1 pound lean ground meat (beef, pork, veal or a combination)	1 egg, beaten
	Salt and pepper to taste
1/2 cup chopped onions	1 cup flour
1/2 cup bread crumbs	1/2 cup vegetable oil
	2 tablespoons ketchup

In a medium bowl, mix together ground meat, onion, bread crumbs, egg and seasonings; roll into golf-ball-sized spheres.

Put flour in a shallow plate and roll meatballs in flour to coat.

In a cast-iron pot over medium-high heat, heat oil. Brown the meatballs in the hot oil, turning frequently to color evenly.

Meanwhile, in a small bowl or cup, blend ketchup with about 1/4 cup water. Add this mixture to the browned meatballs. Reduce heat to low, cover and cook, stirring occasionally, for 20 to 30 minutes, stirring in water as necessary to make a thick dark-brown gravy.

Serve over rice or mashed potatoes.

PORK CHOPS AND RICE

Man cannot live by seafood alone, and pork is another staple in South Louisiana refrigerators and freezers.
Yield: 4 servings

2 tablespoons shortening	2 cloves garlic, finely chopped
4 pork chops	3 1/2 cups chicken broth
1 1/2 teaspoons salt	1 cup uncooked rice
1/4 teaspoon pepper	1 teaspoon powdered thyme,
1/2 cup finely chopped onion	or 2 teaspoons chopped
1/2 cup finely chopped green bell peppers	fresh thyme leaves

Preheat oven to 275°. In a large ovenproof lidded pot or baking dish, melt shortening over medium-high heat. Season pork chops with salt and pepper on both sides. Brown pork chops in shortening about 5 minutes on each side. Remove chops and set aside.

Pour off any excess drippings to leave about 4 tablespoons in pan. Return pan with drippings to burner over medium heat and sauté onions, bell peppers and garlic, stirring frequently, until tender.

Add remaining ingredients; stir well and place chops on top of mixture. Cover and bake at 275° for 30 to 45 minutes, until rice is tender.

BRAISED PORK ROAST

This makes a great traditional-style pot roast and provides great leftover meat for poor-boy sandwiches the next day. Find the biggest Boston butt cut of pork roast available at your grocery store and braise it until it's melt-in-your-mouth tender. If you like, add a pound of sliced potatoes (peeled or unpeeled) and a pound of peeled small finger carrots about 45 minutes before the roast is done.
Yield: 10–12 servings with leftovers

1 large Boston butt pork roast, 6 to 8 pounds	1 tablespoon salt
	1 tablespoon pepper
6 cloves garlic, quartered	1/2 cup oil
4 tablespoons Cajun seasoning	2 cups water

Cut small slits into the roast and insert chunks of garlic. Heavily season the roast with Cajun seasoning, salt and pepper.

In an extra-large heavy pot or Dutch oven with a lid, heat oil over high heat. Brown all sides of the roast in the hot oil.

Reduce heat to medium-low, turn roast fat side up, add water and simmer, covered, for 3 hours or longer, until fork-tender. Remove pot from heat and let sit for at least 15 minunutes before serving.

VENISON STEW

My brother-in-law, Dennis Knight, is a master at making the most of whatever Mother Nature brings his way from hunting and fishing. I've witnessed more than one person enjoying this dish without having any idea they were eating deer meat. Braising (moist-heat cooking) for a long time over low heat will make most any meat tender and flavorful. You can use venison cut from the loin, rump or shank; the shank and rump meat will require longer cooking than the loin.
Yield: 8 servings

1/4 cup vegetable oil
2 to 3 pounds venison, cut into stew-sized chunks
Salt and pepper to taste
12-oz. jar purchased brown gravy, preferably Franco-American
1-ounce packet dry onion-
mushroom soup mix, Lipton's or other
14-oz. can beef broth
1 cup red wine
2 large potatoes, peeled or unpeeled, diced
4 medium carrots, sliced into coins

In a large Dutch oven or cast-iron pot with a lid, heat oil over medium-high heat. Season venison with salt and pepper and brown, uncovered, for 10 to 12 minutes, stirring and turning meat frequently, until chunks are thoroughly and evenly browned.

Reduce heat to medium; add brown gravy, dry soup mix, beef broth and wine; stir to blend well, cover and cook 15 minutes, stirring occasionally.

Add vegetables and more salt and pepper to taste. Liquid should just cover meat and vegetables; add water if necessary. Bring stew back to a simmer, reduce heat to low, cover pot and allow stew to simmer at least 2 hours; 3 or 4 hours would be even better.

Serve over rice or by itself in a bowl.

ARMADILLO FRICASSEE

Cajuns are resourceful people who know how to enjoy whatever fresh meat from a hunt might come their way via friend, relative or neighbor. Thus this armadillo recipe from my Aunt Debbie Reed. It could just as well be possum, raccoon, squirrel or most anything on four legs or two wings. Of course, if you're not feeling adventurous, or it's been a long spell since you've gotten any fresh game from anyone, you can always substitute chicken. That's what you'll say it tastes like anyway.
Yield: 8 servings

2 pounds cleaned armadillo or other meat, chopped into bite-size chunks
Salt and pepper to taste
5 tablespoons roux, made according to instructions on page 9, or dry roux mix
4 large potatoes
5 medium turnips, quartered, optional
1 large onion, chopped
1 green bell pepper, chopped
2 stalks celery, chopped
2 cloves garlic, chopped
1/2 cup chopped green onions
1/4 cup chopped fresh parsley

Heavily season the meat with salt and pepper. If you are using armadillo or other game, place the meat in a lidded pot, cover meat with water, cover pot and bring to a boil, then reduce heat to low and simmer for about an hour. For chicken, this precooking is not necessary.

In a large heavy pot or Dutch oven, dissolve roux in 2 quarts of water. Bring to a boil over medium-high heat; reduce heat to medium-low and simmer, covered, for 30 minutes. Add turnips (if using), onion, bell pepper, celery, garlic, the meat and salt and pepper to taste. Bring back to a boil, reduce to a simmer; cover and cook over medium-low heat about 1 1/2 hours, until meat is tender. Add green onions and parsley during last 20 minutes of cooking.

Serve over cooked rice.

CHICKEN SAUCE PIQUANTE

While gumbo undeniably is the Cajun dish of life, many of my favorite cold-weather memories of growing up in South Louisiana are triggered by the smell of a good sauce piquante cooking on the stove all day in a big iron pot. It's a basic red sauce, crammed with savory vegetables and mouth-watering morsels of meat. In my house, the meat was almost always chicken (my mom made it with bone-in chicken, but my wife and kids prefer boneless thighs). A lot of folks use turtle meat or alligator. It's so good and cooks so long that no one will care what kind of meat you use.
Yield: 10 servings

2/3 cup oil, divided	6 (8-oz.) cans tomato sauce
4 to 5 pounds chicken pieces or boneless thighs	3 (6-oz.) cans tomato paste
Salt and pepper to taste	2 (16-oz.) cans whole tomatoes
4 large onions, chopped	10-oz. can chopped tomatoes and green chiles
6 ribs celery, chopped	4 cups water, divided
1 large green bell pepper, chopped	1 pound sliced fresh button mushrooms
8 green onions, chopped	4 bay leaves
6 cloves garlic, chopped	Cayenne pepper to taste

In a large skillet over a medium-high burner, heat 1/3 cup of the oil. Season chicken with salt and pepper and brown on all sides. Remove and set aside to drain on paper towels.

Meanwhile, in a large Dutch oven or iron pot over a medium-high burner, heat the remaining 1/3 cup of oil and sauté the onions, celery, bell pepper, green onions and garlic, stirring frequently, 10 to 12 minutes, until tender. Stir in the tomato sauce, tomato paste, whole tomatoes, chopped tomatoes and 1 cup of the water; cook, covered, over medium heat for 15 minutes, stirring occasionally. Add chicken, mushrooms, bay leaves and 3 cups of water; bring to a simmer and reduce heat to low. Cook, covered, over low heat, stirring occasionally (mainly so you can lick the spoon and fill your home with the wonderful aroma), at least 2 hours.

STUFFED DUCK BREAST

Even if you don't think you like duck, it's hard not to fall in love with this. It's a delicious dish Cajuns have coveted for generations, and it's a breeze to make on your backyard grill. It's common to find the breasts already stuffed and ready to pop on the grill at grocery stores and meat markets in South Louisiana, but you can find duck breast filets at upscale grocery stores, meat markets and Asian markets in most places. While this dish is best prepared on the grill, you could broil it in your oven, or use an inside smokeless grill, like a George Foreman.

One big tip: if you're using fresh duck breasts, you'll want to marinate the meat in your favorite marinade (we usually use a 16-oz. bottle of Italian dressing) for at least a couple of hours before stuffing it. Marinating overnight is even better.

Yield: 4 servings

4 ounces whipped cream cheese, at room temperature	4 duck breast filets, skin removed, marinated at least 2 hours or overnight in an oil-based marinade
2 tablespoons chopped seeded jalapeño peppers, or to taste	4 slices bacon

Soak 4 toothpicks in water. Prepare coals or preheat gas grill. You will want to cook the duck over a medium-high flame.

Blend cream cheese with chopped jalapeños in a bowl and set aside.

With a thin, sharp knife, starting at one side of the filet, cut a horizontal slit into each breast to form a pocket for the stuffing.

Make the pocket as deep as you can without cutting all the way through the breast on the other side; you don't want to be able to open the filet like a book. After you've cut the pocket into each breast, lay each breast on a work surface, cover it with a sheet of wax paper or plastic wrap, to protect the meat from being torn, and pound the breast lightly with a meat mallet or a heavy-bottomed pan to flatten it evenly to about 1/4-inch thickness. Remove wax paper or plastic wrap. (You could also ask your butcher to cut the pockets into the filets and flatten them slightly.)

Spoon a couple of tablespoons of the cream cheese mixture into the pocket in each breast, then wrap each breast with a slice of bacon and secure the bacon with a toothpick. Grill over medium-high heat for about 20 minutes, turning only once. The duck's ready when the bacon looks cooked.

STUFFED QUAIL

Nephew Brad Stewart in Houma has won multiple 4-H prizes, including one for this recipe — although his bigger claim to fame among my purple-and-gold-loving family and friends is that he won a spot in the legendary Fighting Tiger marching band at LSU.

The brining step makes these little guys more tender and succulent. Chefs often use aromatics such as orange peel or chunks of ginger in their brines — feel free to experiment if you're so moved.

Bertha's Best Cornbread Dressing makes a great stuffing (you can omit the oysters and even the chicken to simplify it), but any cornbread dressing will do.

If you're lucky enough to have a mess of doves on hand, this would work for them, too.

Yield: 8–10 servings

Brine:

2 cups salt

2 quarts water

Birds:

16 whole quail, cleaned and dressed

Salt, pepper and cayenne pepper to taste

4 cups Bertha's Best Cornbread Dressing, page 68, oysters and chicken optional

16 slices of bacon

1.5-oz. package dry onion soup mix

1/2 cup chopped onion

1/2 cup chopped celery

10.5-oz. can beef consommé

Parsley sprigs and lemon wedges for garnish

Brine:

In a nonreactive pot or other container big enough to hold the water and the quail — a scrupulously clean plastic bucket works well — stir the salt into the water until dissolved. Soak birds in the brine for 30 minutes.

Birds:

Preheat oven to 350°. Rinse birds thoroughly and season inside and out with salt, pepper and cayenne. Spoon about 1/4 cup cornbread dressing inside each bird and wrap each with a slice of bacon. Place in roasting pan, breast side up. Sprinkle with onion soup mix, onion and celery. Pour beef consommé over all and bake, uncovered, for 1 1/2 hours. Baste frequently with the juices in the pan, adding water if the pan gets too dry. When done, remove from oven, allow to sit for 5 minutes, garnish with parsley sprigs and lemon wedges and serve hot.

Side Dishes and Salads

ARTICHOKE CASSEROLE

This is another dish that always turned up at potluck dinners. You'd rarely spot it on any of the children's plates, but the adults ate it up.
Yield: 3–4 servings

15-oz. can green beans, drained
15-oz. can artichoke hearts, drained and chopped
3/4 cup Italian-seasoned bread crumbs
1/2 cup grated Parmesan cheese
2 cloves garlic, chopped
5 drops lemon juice
2 teaspoons olive oil
Salt and pepper to taste

Preheat oven to 325° and grease a 1-quart baking dish. Combine all ingredients in prepared baking dish and bake for 20 minutes.

CABBAGE STIR-FRY

I was hesitant to try this dish initially, because it's cooked cabbage — another plentiful home garden crop in South Louisiana, and one I didn't love as a child. But now I look forward to the times when my wife, Suzanne, makes it.
Yield: 6–8 servings

1/4 cup oil
1 small onion, chopped finely
1 large cabbage, washed, shredded
1/2 pound diced ham
Cajun seasoning to taste

In a large skillet, heat oil over medium heat and cook onions in oil, stirring occasionally, until wilted.

Reduce heat to medium-low, mix in remaining ingredients and stir often until heated through.

CORN RELISH

This relish recipe is from my Grandma Reed. It's much better if you prepare it the night before.
Yield: 8–10 servings

15-oz. can whole-kernel corn, drained	2 tablespoons drained canned pimiento, minced
2 stalks celery, chopped finely	1/3 cup corn oil
1/2 green bell pepper, chopped finely	2 tablespoons vinegar
1 small onion, chopped finely	1 teaspoon dry mustard
	1 teaspoon salt
	1 teaspoon sugar

In a medium bowl, mix together corn, celery, bell pepper, onion and pimiento.

In a separate small bowl, thoroughly whisk together remaining ingredients.

Cover both bowls and refrigerate overnight. The next day, combine the contents of the two bowls, mix thoroughly and transfer to serving dish.

MAQUE CHOUX (STEWED CORN)

This is a side dish you'll want again and again. Cajuns serve it as a side dish to most anything. One of the world's great restaurants, Prejean's in Lafayette, puts a spoonful of maque choux in a miniature sweet pie crust as a side dish on many of its entrees.

Yield: 8–10 servings

1 stick (1/2 cup) butter or margarine	1 clove garlic, minced
1 large onion, chopped	6 to 8 ears fresh corn, shucked and silked, or 2 pounds frozen corn kernels
1 large green bell pepper, chopped	
1 large fresh tomato, diced small (or a 10.75-oz. can diced tomatoes)	1 1/2 cups half-and-half
	1 tablespoon Cajun seasoning
	1 teaspoon white pepper
	Hot-pepper sauce to taste

In a deep, large skillet or heavy pot over medium heat, melt the butter and cook the onion, bell pepper, tomato and garlic in it, stirring occasionally, until tender. Meanwhile, if using fresh corn, cut the kernels from the cobs into a large bowl.

Add the corn, half-and-half, Cajun seasoning and white pepper to the pot, along with a couple dashes of hot sauce if you want it spicier. Stir to blend; reduce heat to low and simmer uncovered over low heat for at least 1 hour, stirring occasionally.

BERTHA'S BEST CORNBREAD DRESSING

This is a holiday favorite of my brother-in-law, Dennis Knight, whose grandmother, Bertha Knight, handed the recipe down to him. Dennis loves oysters in almost anything. If you don't, the dressing is still delicious without them; just don't tell Dennis.
Yield: 8–10 servings

Seasoning mix:

2 teaspoons salt	1/2 teaspoon onion powder
1 1/2 teaspoons ground white pepper	1/2 teaspoon thyme
1 teaspoon crushed red pepper	1/4 teaspoon dried oregano

Dressing:

1/2 cup butter
3/4 cup chopped onions
3/4 cup chopped green bell
    pepper
1/2 cup chopped celery
1 tablespoon minced garlic
2 bay leaves
2 cups chicken broth
1 tablespoon Tabasco sauce
5 cups crumbled cornbread

(see Cajun Cornbread
    recipe, page 79)
4 slices toasted white or other
    bread, crumbled
3 cups coarsely chopped
    cooked chicken breast
1 pint drained raw oysters
4 hard-cooked eggs, sliced
    thinly
3 raw eggs, beaten

Seasoning mix:

Combine ingredients thoroughly in a small bowl and set aside.

Dressing:

Preheat oven to 350°. Grease a 4-quart baking dish.

Melt butter over medium heat in a deep 12-inch heavy skillet. When melted, raise heat to high and add onions, bell pepper, celery, garlic and bay leaves. Cook over high heat for about 3 minutes, stirring almost constantly to keep mixture from burning. Lower heat to medium-high, add seasoning mix and cook, stirring frequently, for 5 additional minutes. Stir in chicken broth and Tabasco; cook, stirring occasionally, another 5 minutes over medium-high heat. Turn off heat and remove skillet from burner.

Add cornbread and toasted bread, chicken, oysters, hard-cooked and raw eggs. Mix lightly but thoroughly. Spoon into prepared baking dish and bake uncovered at 350° until nicely browned on top, about 1 hour and 15 minutes.

CINDY'S BEST EGGPLANT CASSEROLE

A good year in the vegetable garden can mean a lot *of eggplants. My sister-in-law Cindy Knight and her husband Dennis sometimes get bagfuls from their back yard. Here's what Cindy does with some of them — I've seen plenty of non-eggplant-eaters dig into this dish.*
Yield: 8–10 servings

4 large black eggplants
3 pounds large Louisiana
   shrimp
1 cup diced onions
1 cup diced celery
1/2 cup diced banana pepper
6 cloves garlic, minced
1 stick (1/2 cup) butter
2 tablespoons parsley flakes
1/2 teaspoon black pepper

1/2 teaspoon Morton
   Season-All salt
Dash of Tabasco sauce, or
   more to taste
1/2 cup grated Parmesan
   cheese
3 to 5 cups seasoned bread
   crumbs
1/2 cup shredded mozzarella
   cheese

Preheat oven to 400°. Wrap each whole eggplant in aluminum foil. Place wrapped eggplants in oven and bake for 35 to 45 minutes, until eggplants are soft. Remove and let cool.

Meanwhile, prepare other ingredients: Peel shrimp and set aside in separate bowl; dice onions, celery and banana pepper and combine in a separate bowl. Mince garlic and set aside for later.

Melt butter over medium heat in large skillet or 6-quart Dutch oven. Add onion, celery and banana pepper, sauté, stirring occasionally, until onions are clear.

Remove foil from eggplant; use a paring knife to peel off skin and discard. Cut flesh into strips or cubes and add to onion mixture. Add garlic and stir to blend. Reduce heat to low and simmer, uncovered, for about 15 minutes, stirring occasionally to keep mixture from burning.

Add shrimp, cover and continue cooking for about 10 minutes;

then add parsley, black pepper, Season-All salt, Tabasco and Parmesan cheese.

Remove pan from heat; preheat oven to 400° and grease a large casserole dish.

Gently and gradually start folding bread crumbs into the eggplant mixture, a little at a time, until mixture is thickened. Be careful not to add too many bread crumbs; this will make the mixture too pasty. Reserve enough bread crumbs to sprinkle over the top. Add Tabasco to taste, if you want the casserole spicier.

Transfer this mixture into the greased casserole dish. Spread mozzarella over the top and sprinkle a light layer of bread crumbs atop. Bake 20 to 30 minutes, until top is browned and casserole is bubbly. Let cool a few minutes before serving.

OKRA AND CORN

Cajun gardeners often have a lot of success growing okra — and that means finding creative ways to prepare it. You can only freeze so much to use in the winter in gumbo. Here's a dish my sister-in-law Cindy Knight came up with.

Fresh corn kernels are best, of course (slice them off the cob into a large bowl and then "milk" the cob by pressing the dull edge of your knife down it all the way around), but frozen or canned will work fine too.

Yield: 6–7 servings

4 tablespoons melted butter
1 cup thinly sliced okra
4 teaspoons lemon juice
2 tablespoons flour
2 cups fresh corn kernels with their "milk," or 15-oz. can

corn kernels, or frozen corn kernels, thawed
1 cup milk
8 ounces shredded sharp Cheddar cheese
1 cup plain bread crumbs

Preheat oven to 350° and grease a 9-by-12-inch casserole dish.

Melt butter in 12-inch skillet over medium-high heat; add okra and lemon juice (it helps the texture of the okra) and cook, stirring frequently, for about 5 minutes. Lower heat to medium and add flour; stir for a few minutes more to take raw taste out of flour. Add corn kernels, milk and cheese. Stir well and cook until cheese is melted.

Pour into greased casserole dish, sprinkle bread crumbs on top and bake at 350° for about 45 minutes, until browned and bubbly.

DIRTY RICE

My mom's rice dressing remains a much-requested side dish for holiday feasts, especially Thanksgiving and Christmas. It remains popular after decades of special dinners. It's great as a leftover.
Yield: 8–10 servings

1/2 cup vegetable oil	1/2 teaspoon powdered thyme
1/2 pound ground beef (or use part ground beef and part ground pork)	1/4 teaspoon ground red pepper
	1 bay leaf
Finely chopped gizzards and liver from 1 turkey or 2 fryer chickens, optional	2 cups uncooked rice
	4 cups water
	1 tablespoon butter, optional
1 large onion, chopped	2 teaspoons salt
1 green bell pepper, chopped	3 green onions, chopped
2 stalks celery, chopped	1/4 cup minced fresh parsley
2 teaspoons salt	

In a large lidded cast-iron Dutch oven or pot, heat oil over medium heat and cook ground meat and chopped gizzards (if using) until browned, stirring often. Add onion, bell pepper and celery. Cook, stirring often, over medium heat until onions are transparent. Add salt, thyme, red pepper, bay leaf and chopped liver (if using).

Raise heat to high, bring to a boil, reduce heat to low and

simmer, covered, for 30 minutes over low heat. When done, there should be about 1/2 cup of liquid left from juices given off by meat and vegetables; add water if necessary.

While meat mixture is simmering, cook the rice with the water, butter (if using) and salt in a separate pot or rice cooker while preparing the other ingredients (see "How to make rice" on page 10). Keep rice covered until needed.

When meat mixture is done, remove the bay leaf and stir in the freshly cooked rice, then the green onions and parsley. Remove from heat, cover and let stand 10 minutes before serving.

ZUCCHINI PIROGUES

If you have a bumper crop of zucchini, this is a great recipe for a down-the-bayou version of zucchini boats. Pirogues are flat-bottomed Cajun canoes. Where I grew up, it was common for kids to have bicycles to get around on land and pirogues to paddle around on the bayou. When scooped out and ready to be stuffed for this dish, the zucchini resemble miniature dugout canoes. This is one recipe where small zucchini aren't the best choice; you want them big enough to hold a reasonable amount of stuffing.
Yield: 4–6 servings

2 1/4 teaspoons salt, divided
4 zucchini
2 tablespoons olive oil
1 medium onion, chopped
3/4 cup chopped button mushrooms
1 clove garlic, minced
2 cups diced fresh tomatoes
2 tablespoons chopped fresh parsley

1/4 teaspoon Cajun seasoning
Ground black pepper to taste
1/3 cup bread crumbs
1/4 cup grated Parmesan cheese
3 tablespoons finely chopped tasso (see "Ingredients and cooking terms," page 14) or crisp-cooked bacon

Fill an 8-quart soup pot halfway with water and add 2 teaspoons of the salt. Bring to a boil over high heat; when water is at a full boil, add the whole zucchini and let them boil for 1 1/2 minutes – just long enough to soften the skin. Remove zucchini with tongs and place in a colander to drain.

When squash are cool enough to handle, cut each in half lengthwise and scoop out some of the central flesh with a spoon, leaving an outer wall at least 1/3-inch thick. Finely chop the scooped-out flesh and set aside.

In a 10-inch sauté pan, heat the oil over medium heat; add the onion and the chopped zucchini flesh and sauté over medium heat, stirring, for 5 minutes. Add the mushrooms and garlic and sauté, stirring, for another 2 minutes. Add the tomatoes and turn up the heat to medium-high. Bring the mixture to a low boil and let boil for about 3 minutes, just until the tomatoes are soft.

Remove the pan from heat and stir in the parsley, the remaining 1/4 teaspoon of salt, the Cajun seasoning and pepper to taste. Let the vegetables cool for 4 to 5 minutes, then add the bread crumbs, Parmesan and tasso or bacon.

Preheat oven to 400° and grease a shallow 2-1/2-to-3-quart baking dish with vegetable oil.

Spoon the filling into the zucchini halves and place the zucchini in the baking dish. Bake on center oven rack for 25 min.; serve immediately.

SLICED CUCUMBER AND TOMATO SALAD

If it was a good season for tomatoes, cucumbers and other garden vegetables, this is something that would be on the dinner table night after night. There's nothing like picking vegetables right off the vine and serving them fresh. My dad, Lloyd, would eat tomatoes off the vine as you would an apple while he was working in the garden. My brothers and I loved the tomatoes and cucumbers but weren't as thrilled if there was a bumper crop of beets or eggplant or mirlitons (a relative of squash and cucumbers, also known as

chayote or vegetable pears). This salad can be prepared in advance and allowed to chill overnight.
Yield: 4–6 servings

4 fresh cucumbers, peeled and sliced into rounds	4 fresh tomatoes, sliced
1 medium red onion, sliced thinly	1/2 (16-oz.) bottle Italian dressing
	Salt and pepper to taste

Mix all ingredients in a large bowl and refrigerate for at least an hour.

CUCUMBER, ONION AND SOUR CREAM SALAD

Here's another simple, fresh vegetable dish that takes advantage of the summer garden harvest. This can be made a day in advance.
Yield: 6–8 servings

2 cucumbers	Pinch of chopped fresh mint, or more to taste
1/4 cup red onion, sliced thinly	1 cup sour cream
1/4 cup green onions, sliced thinly	Salt and pepper

Peel, quarter and slice the cucumbers into small chunks. Add the red onion, green onion and mint, then fold in the sour cream and salt and pepper and chill for at least an hour before serving.

POTATO SALAD

There are as many variations of potato salad as there are ways to catch an alligator, and every version any relative or friend of mine makes is good. I'm happy for some variety, but not everyone is open-minded about potato salad. Some peel the potatoes; some don't. Mayonnaise? Mustard? Or both? Here's a basic version that has mustard and mayonnaise. Put your own twist on it. Potato salad, like hot French bread, is meant to accompany almost any dish. Some folks even like a scoop of potato salad in the middle of a steaming bowl of gumbo.
Yield: 6–8 servings

6 medium potatoes, boiled, diced
1 medium onion, chopped finely
2 stalks celery, chopped finely
4 green onions with tops, chopped finely
4 hard-cooked eggs, peeled and chopped finely
1 cup mayonnaise
1/4 cup pickle relish
2 tablespoons mustard, or more to taste (yellow is fine, but you can use another kind)
Salt and pepper to taste
Chopped fresh parsley and paprika, for garnish

Combine first eight ingredients in a large bowl and mix well. Add more mustard if preferred. Season to taste with salt and pepper. Garnish as desired with parsley and paprika.

REED RICE SALAD

This is one of the recipes my Aunt Charlotte and Uncle Ron Hewitt collected when the family was marketing Reed Rice, from the family farm near Iota, as a premium brand.
Yield: 6–8 servings

3 cups cooked white rice, cooled
4 hard-cooked eggs, peeled and chopped
1/2 cup mayonnaise
1/2 cup chopped black olives
1/4 cup chopped onion
1/4 cup chopped green bell pepper
1/4 cup chopped celery
1 teaspoon yellow mustard
Salt and pepper to taste

In a large bowl, blend all ingredients together gently but thoroughly. Chill for at least an hour before serving.

WATERGATE SALAD (AKA FLUFF)

I've never seen a buffet spread back home without some variation of "fluff," also known as ambrosia or Watergate salad. It's good stuff, fluff. This variation comes from a daughter of a cousin, Amanda Trahan.
Yield: 8–10 servings

20-oz. can crushed pineapple
3/4 cup mini marshmallows
1/2 cup chopped pecans
9-oz. container of frozen whipped topping, thawed
3-oz. package instant pistachio pudding mix

Combine all ingredients in large mixing bowl, cover and chill for at least 30 minutes.

Breads

PAIN ORDINAIRE

French bread goes with everything, and while it's convenient to grab at the grocery store, it's even better made at home. One side benefit: the fabulous aroma. Another: The more bread you make, the more you have leftover for bread pudding, French toast and other dishes.
Yield: 2 loaves

.25-oz. package active dry yeast
2 cups warm water (about 110°), divided
1 1/2 teaspoons salt

5 cups all-purpose flour, plus more for flouring board
2 tablespoons butter, divided
1/4 cup milk

In a large mixing bowl, dissolve the yeast in 1/4 cup of the warm water. Add salt and the remaining 1 3/4 cups of water; mix. Gradually stir in flour to make a dough.

Turn dough onto floured board and knead for 10 minutes, until dough becomes smooth and elastic. Grease a large mixing bowl with half the butter; place the dough in the bowl and cover with a damp towel. Let the covered dough rise in a warm place about 2 hours, until its bulk roughly doubles. Punch the dough down and let it sit until it doubles again; then turn out onto floured board and knead lightly.

Shape dough into 2 long loaves. Grease a large baking sheet with the remaining tablespoon of butter; place loaves on sheet and leave covered in a warm place until they double in size.

When the loaves are about half-risen, cut a few diagonal slits across the top of each and brush the surfaces with the milk. Preheat oven to 400°. When loaves have risen, uncover and bake at 400° about 20 to 25 minutes, until golden.

A Cajun technique: Placing a small pan of boiling water at the bottom of the oven will produce a heavier crust.

CAJUN CORNBREAD

Man does not live by white bread alone. Cornbread goes great with soups, stews and so many other Cajun dishes. Here's a good basic cornbread recipe that works well in cornbread dressings. The onion and the jalapeños add the extra oomph that Cajuns require.

1/4 cup shortening (Crisco or bacon grease)	2 eggs, slightly beaten
1 cup yellow cornmeal	3/4 cup milk
1 cup flour	1/4 cup whipping cream
2 tablespoons sugar	1/2 cup finely chopped onion
1 tablespoon baking powder	3 jalapeño peppers, seeds and veins removed, chopped
1/2 teaspoon salt	into medium chunks

Preheat oven to 425°. Put shortening in a 10-inch cast-iron skillet and place the skillet in the oven to preheat it and to liquefy the shortening.

Into a medium bowl, sift together cornmeal, flour, sugar, baking powder and salt. Stir in eggs, milk and whipping cream; then stir in onion and jalapeños.

Remove skillet from oven (be careful; it's really hot); swirl shortening around in skillet to coat the sides and then pour the shortening into the batter and mix in with a few strokes. Pour batter into the skillet and bake at 425° about 20 minutes, until golden and firmly set. Bake 5 or 10 minutes longer if you like a dark-brown crust.

MOLASSES CORNBREAD

South Louisiana is known for its abundant seafood, rice, fruits and vegetables, but don't forget the sugar cane and sugar mills. One of my favorite fall harvest memories is the pungent smell of bagasse (raw sugar residue) from the sugar mills. Having a vibrant sugar industry in South Louisiana meant ample supplies of pure cane syrups and molasses. Here's a variation of cornbread that takes advantage of that.

Yield: 4–6 servings

1 cup flour	1/4 cup molasses
3/4 cup cornmeal	1 cup milk
2 teaspoons baking powder	1 egg, well beaten
3/4 teaspoon salt	2 tablespoons cooking oil

Preheat oven to 425°. In a medium mixing bowl, sift together the flour, cornmeal, baking powder and salt. Stir in the molasses, then the milk and beaten egg.

In an 8-by-8-inch baking pan, heat the oil, either on a medium-high burner or in the preheating oven. When the oil is hot (be careful not to burn yourself with the hot pan), pour it from the hot pan into the cornmeal mixture. Don't be alarmed — it will bubble. Stir to blend. Pour the cornbread mixture into the hot greased pan (this will help make a nice crust) and bake at 425° for about 20 minutes, until browned.

HUSH PUPPIES

Cajuns typically whip up a batch of these crispy cornmeal treats to go with fried seafood, but you can fry them in a pan with oil anytime you like. You can use a deep-fryer for these, but I prefer to use a heavy 12-inch skillet. You can use peanut, safflower or canola oil for frying; if you're using a skillet, you'll need enough oil to come about halfway up the puppies' sides. You want a temperature of 350° to 375°; if you don't have a thermometer, drop a kernel of popcorn into the oil; when it pops, the oil is hot enough. The ideal scenario is to fry the patties in the still-hot oil from the batch of fish or shrimp you just fried.

Yield: about a dozen hush puppies

Oil for frying	**Cayenne pepper** to taste
1 cup yellow cornmeal	**1 small onion,** chopped finely
2 teaspoons baking powder	**1 egg**
1/2 teaspoon salt	**1/4 cup milk**

Begin heating oil in a deep-fryer or 12-inch heavy skillet.

In a large mixing bowl, mix together all the dry ingredients and the chopped onion. Break in the egg and beat briskly. Add milk and mix gently and thoroughly.

Form the dough into round, slightly flattened golf-ball-sized patties about 1 1/2 inches in diameter; if you press a small hole in the center of each puppy with your finger or thumb, it will keep the center from becoming too heavy and will give you a larger crunchy surface. Alternatively, you can skip hand-forming the puppies and simply drop the dough into the hot oil. Either way, you don't want to crowd the pan, because that will lower the temperature of the oil and the puppies will absorb the oil and won't cook up crisp.

Fry the hush puppies, turning if necessary to brown evenly, about 3 to 4 minutes, until crisp and golden-brown; serve hot.

BANANA-PINEAPPLE NUT BREAD

This is a tasty recipe from my Aunt Nell Stephens, who moved at a young age to a place that many of my relatives consider "up north"— Natchitoches, La.
Yield: 2 loaves

3 cups all-purpose flour
2 cups sugar
1 teaspoon baking soda
1 teaspoon salt
1 teaspoon ground cinnamon
1 cup chopped nuts

3 eggs, well beaten
2 cups mashed ripe bananas
1 1/2 cups vegetable oil
8-oz. can crushed pineapple,
    drained; syrup discarded
2 teaspoons vanilla extract

Preheat oven to 350°. Grease and flour 2 9-by-5-by-3-inch loaf pans.

In a large mixing bowl, combine flour, sugar, baking soda, salt and cinnamon. Stir in nuts.

In a separate medium bowl, combine remaining ingredients, mixing thoroughly to blend; then add to dry ingredients, stirring just until moist.

Divide batter between prepared loaf pans. Bake at 350° for 1 hour, or until browned. Allow bread to cool 10 minutes before removing loaves from pans.

PEANUT BUTTER BREAD

This is a Reed family recipe from my Aunt Debbie, and it could just as well be a dessert. Reeds love their sweets, and they love almost anything with peanut butter.
Yield: 1 loaf

2 cups all-purpose flour	3/4 cup creamy or crunchy
1/2 cup sugar	peanut butter
2 teaspoons baking powder	1 large egg
1 teaspoon salt	1 cup milk

Preheat oven to 350°. Grease a 9-by-5-inch loaf pan.

In a medium mixing bowl, stir together dry ingredients. Cut in the peanut butter with a fork or pastry blender until crumbly.

In a separate small bowl, beat egg and stir in milk to blend; stir this mixture into the dry ingredients and mix just until moistened.

Pour batter into greased pan. Bake at 350° for 1 hour, or until a wooden toothpick inserted into the center comes out clean. Remove loaf from pan immediately and cool on a wire rack.

Desserts

PRALINES

This is one of my most cherished recipes from my mom. She always taught me that it's best to make pralines on cold, sunny days with low humidity. Unless you're an experienced cook who knows how to tell when a mixture is heated to precisely the "soft-ball" stage, use a candy thermometer.
Yield: 10–12 servings

2 cups sugar
1 stick (1/2 cup) butter or
    margarine
16 large marshmallows

1/2 cup evaporated milk
2 cups whole pecans
1 teaspoon vanilla extract

Line 2 cookie sheets with waxed paper.

In a heavy pot, stir together all ingredients except pecans and vanilla. Cook, stirring frequently, for about 3 minutes over medium heat; then stir in pecans and continue cooking until mixture is heated to the soft ball stage (235°, or when a bit of the mixture, dropped into cold water, forms a soft ball).

Remove from heat; add vanilla extract and beat with a wooden spoon until the mixture takes on a dull look. Drop by spoonfuls onto waxed-paper-lined cookie sheets, spacing the pralines far enough apart to allow them to spread, and let them cool.

PECAN PRALINE GOODIES

Here's a quick, easy recipe from my Cousin Kristy Reed. If "praline" is in the title of a recipe, it's got to be good. I must say, the Reed family knows its sweets.
Yield: 8–10 servings

Enough graham crackers to cover a cookie sheet in one layer	**2 sticks (1 cup) butter or margarine**
	1/2 cup sugar
	1 cup chopped pecans

Preheat oven to 350°. Tear off enough waxed paper to approximate the size of the cookie sheet you will be using and set it aside on your counter.

Lay graham crackers out on the cookie sheet in one layer, sides touching, so that they completely cover the cookie sheet.
In a small saucepan, bring butter and sugar to a full boil. Pour the mixture over the graham crackers on the cookie sheet, covering completely. Sprinkle with chopped pecans.

Bake at 350° for 8-10 minutes. Remove from oven and immediately slide the whole shebang from the cookie sheet onto the waxed paper to cool. When candy is cool, break it into pieces.

PEANUT BUTTER FUDGE

This recipe, which my mom always made for the Christmas holidays, can spark so many childhood memories for me: Fighting my brothers over who got to lick the spoon and the bowl (my son, Nick, gets that honor now). My mom trying to hide the fudge from my dad, but my dad always finding it. The neighborhood kids trying to sneak a piece every chance they got.

Again, it's smart to use a candy thermometer with this one.
Yield: 12 servings

1 cup milk	1/2 pint marshmallow creme
3 cups sugar	1 teaspoon vanilla extract
1 cup peanut butter	

Grease a 12-inch square baking pan.

In a saucepan over a medium burner, heat milk until very hot but not boiling.

Put sugar in a large mixing bowl, add hot milk to sugar and mix well.

Pour mixture into a saucepan and cook over medium heat, without stirring, until it reaches the soft-ball stage (235°, or when a bit of the mixture, dropped into cold water, forms a soft ball). Remove from heat and pour back into bowl.

Add peanut butter, marshmallow creme and vanilla extract and beat briefly. When mixture begins to thicken, pour into greased pan and let cool.

PEANUT BUTTER QUICKIES

Here's another great peanut-butter recipe from my mom.
Yield: 8–10 servings

10-oz. can condensed milk	2 cups fine graham cracker
1/2 cup creamy peanut butter	crumbs
	1/2 cup pitted dates, chopped

Preheat oven to 325° and grease a cookie sheet. In medium mixing bowl, blend milk and peanut butter until smooth. Mix in graham crumbs and dates.

Drop by teaspoonfuls 1 inch apart onto greased cookie sheet. Bake at 325° for 12 minutes or until light brown; be careful not to overbake, as they will get too hard.

MANDY'S REED RICE PUDDING

Back when the Reeds marketed their rice as a premium product that was lightly milled to be better for your health, this was one of the delightful recipes my Aunt Charlotte Hewitt came up with.
Yield: 8 servings

2 tablespoons butter, divided	1/2 teaspoon ground cinnamon
1/2 cup washed, uncooked rice	1/2 teaspoon ground nutmeg
4 cups milk	1/2 teaspoon salt
1/2 cup golden raisins	Whipped cream for topping,
1/2 cup honey	to taste

Preheat oven to 300° and grease a 2-quart casserole with 1 tablespoon of the butter.

In a large bowl, thoroughly mix together rice, milk, raisins, honey, cinnamon, nutmeg and salt.

Pour mixture into greased casserole dish. Bake at 300° for 2 hours, stirring every 15 minutes. When the pudding has only 15 minutes left to bake, remove from oven, dot with the remaining tablespoon of butter and return to oven for final 15 minutes.

Serve warm, topped with whipped cream.

BREAD PUDDING

There are almost as many variations of bread pudding as there are cooks — and that's a lot, in Cajun country. Here's a good, basic version from my Aunt Debbie Reed. French bread is traditional here, but any bread will work. Whatever kind you use, there is no better way on earth to make use of stale bread!
Yield: 8 servings

12-oz. can evaporated milk	1 1/2 cups sugar
2 1/2 cups water	1 teaspoon vanilla extract
About 10 slices of bread	3 to 4 tablespoons butter or
(slightly stale is best)	margarine, melted
3 eggs	1/4 cup raisins

Preheat oven to 300° and coat a 13-by-9-by-2-inch pan with vegetable oil spray.

In a medium saucepan, mix together the evaporated milk and water. Place on a burner over medium heat, stirring constantly to keep the milk from burning or boiling. Just before it comes to a boil, remove from heat and pour into a large bowl.

Tear bread into chunks and add to evaporated-milk mixture. Set aside and let soak while preparing the rest of the recipe.

Into a separate bowl, break eggs 1 at a time, beating briefly after each addition. Stir in sugar. Add vanilla, melted butter and raisins. Stir and then pour over the soaked bread, stirring the bread gently to mix.

Pour into prepared pan and bake at 300° for 45 to 50 minutes.

SWEET POTATO PUDDING

Try it; you'll like it. The Reed family knows good home cooking in general, but making scrumptious sweets is a special Reed strength. This recipe from my Aunt Nell Stephens in Natchitoches stars an ingredient that's in abundant supply in fall and winter. It's delicious served either hot or cold.
Yield: 6–8 servings

3 cups peeled, grated raw
   sweet potatoes
1 1/2 cups evaporated milk (or
   regular milk)
1 cup firmly packed light-
   brown sugar
2 eggs, beaten

1/3 cup butter, melted
1 tablespoon ground cinnamon
   OR 1 teaspoon ground
   nutmeg, optional
1 teaspoon vanilla
1/2 teaspoon salt

Preheat oven to 350°. Grease a shallow baking dish.

In a large mixing bowl, mix together all ingredients. Transfer to greased baking dish and bake at 350° for about 1 hour, until pudding is set and top is browned.

SOUR CREAM POUND CAKE

This rich pound cake from my grandmother Pearl Reed was scrumptious by itself but also served as the base for many other classic desserts, most memorably strawberry shortcake. We also loved it a la mode with vanilla ice cream, or simply topped with a generous amount of hot fudge or butterscotch.
Yield: 8–10 servings

2 sticks (1 cup) butter, softened to room temperature (do not substitute light butter or margarine)
3 cups sugar
3 cups sifted cake flour
6 eggs
1/4 teaspoon salt
1 1/2 teaspoons vanilla extract
1/2 teaspoon lemon extract
1/4 teaspoon ground nutmeg
8 ounces sour cream

Preheat oven to 325°. Grease and flour a tube cake pan.

In bowl of electric mixer, cream butter on low speed. With mixer running, add sugar; then flour, 1/3 cup at a time. Next, add eggs, one at a time, mixing well after each addition. Add salt and flavorings, then sour cream, mixing thoroughly.

Pour into prepared tube cake pan. Bake 30 minutes at 325°; reduce heat to 300° and bake 1 hour more.

FIG CAKE

Here's a recipe from Grandma Reed that takes advantage of the summer bounty of local fig trees.
Yield: 8 servings

1 quart figs
2 cups plus 6 tablespoons of
   flour
2 tablespoons sugar
2 teaspoons baking powder
2 teaspoons baking soda
2 teaspoons salt

2 eggs
1 cup vegetable oil
2 tablespoons vanilla extract
1 cup chopped pecans and/or
   1/2 cup chopped dates may
   be added; both are optional

Preheat oven to 350°. Grease and flour a large bundt cake pan.

Chop figs roughly and then mash them to a puree with a fork, or whirl them briefly in a food processor.

In a large mixing bowl, stir together flour, sugar, baking powder, baking soda and salt to blend well.

In a separate bowl, beat eggs; then add oil, vanilla and mashed figs. Mix thoroughly. Stir in pecans and/or dates, if using. Add this mixture to the dry ingredients, stir to blend well and pour into prepared bundt pan. Bake at 350° for 1 hour.

PIÑA COLADA CAKE

This was one of my mom's favorite sheet cake recipes; it was passed around Cajun kitchens for years. She often made it when she was asked to bring dessert to a potluck dinner or family gathering. Leave off the coconut if some of your guests don't like it.
Yield: 8-10 servings

18.25-oz. box yellow cake mix	8-oz. container frozen
15-oz. can Coco Lopez piña colada mix	whipped topping, thawed
14-oz. can sweetened condensed milk	1/2 cup flaked coconut, optional

Mix cake and bake as directed in a 13-by-9-inch cake pan.

While cake is baking, in a medium mixing bowl, stir together piña colada mix and condensed milk. Mixture should be the consistency of a thin pudding.

Remove cake from oven. With a skewer, punch several holes in the cake while it's hot and pour the mixture slowly over the cake. Let cool. To serve, top with whipped topping and coconut, if using.

HERSHEY BAR PIE

My Grandma Reed used to make this rich, dreamy and easy dessert on the farm in Iota. It never lasted long.
Yield: 8 servings

6 Hershey's milk-chocolate bars, 1.55-oz. each	1 graham-cracker pie crust
10 large marshmallows	12-oz. container frozen whipped topping, thawed
1/4 cup milk	

Melt chocolate bars in a large microwave-safe container in microwave, cooking on defrost setting for 4 to 5 minutes. Stir to finish melting. Fold in marshmallows and blend until marshmallows have melted. Thoroughly mix in milk.

Pour mixture into crust, cover with clear plastic wrap and refrigerate overnight. Top with whipped topping and serve.

PECAN PIE

Baking up dozens of small-sized pecan pies is a decades-long holiday tradition of my mother-in-law, Helen Roy. To keep them from disappearing too quickly, she hides some from her three grandsons. Helen is a believer in keeping it simple, so she uses pre-made pie shells. Depending on the occasion, she makes either one full-sized pie or 16 small ones. In the store, pecan pieces are usually cheaper, and they're fine for this recipe, but the more expensive pecan halves make for a much prettier pie.
Yield: 8 servings

3 eggs	1 cup sugar
1/2 cup Karo or other light corn syrup	1 tablespoon flour
	Dash of salt
1 teaspoon vanilla	9-inch pie shell, or 16
1 cup pecan halves or pieces	miniature pie shells

Preheat oven to 350°. In a large mixing bowl, beat eggs, then stir in syrup, vanilla, pecans and sugar, mixing well to blend. Mix in flour and salt. Spoon into pie shell(s); if using small pie shells, use roughly 3 iced-tea spoons of filling each. Bake at 350° for 30 to 35 minutes, until top is golden.

ICE CREAM ROLL

Here's one last classic from the Reed family vault. It's a special dessert my Cousin Connie Trahan has been making for her father, my Uncle Norman Reed, for as long as any of us can remember. He was always partial to vanilla ice cream in the dish.
Yield: 6–8 servings

4 eggs, separated	3/4 teaspoon baking powder
3/4 cup sugar	Confectioners' sugar for sifting
1 teaspoon vanilla extract	1/2 gallon ice cream, any flavor
3/4 cup flour	

Preheat oven to 375° and grease a rimmed cookie sheet or jellyroll pan.

In a medium mixing bowl, beat egg yolks until light; add sugar gradually and beat until creamy. Mix in vanilla.

Into a separate bowl, sift flour with baking powder; then add gradually to egg mixture; beating until smooth.

In a separate bowl, whip egg whites until stiff but not dry; fold into cake batter. Pour mixture onto greased cookie sheet and bake at 375° for 13 minutes. Remove from oven and dust the top of the cake heavily with confectioners' sugar. Cover the sheet with a clean white dish towel with a smooth weave (not terrycloth). Grasp the cookie sheet by both ends, keeping the towel stretched firmly over the sheet cake. Gently turn the pan with the cake upside down and place it, towel down, on the counter; then gently lift the pan to release the cake so it is sitting on the towel.

Let the cake sit for about 3 minutes. Then, starting with one of the short ends, gently roll the sheet of cake up into a cylinder and wrap the cylinder in plastic wrap to help it hold its spiral shape while cooling completely. When cake is cool, remove the plastic wrap, place it back on the cookie sheet and carefully unroll it.

Microwave ice cream on low power in 30-second increments, checking after each, until it is softened just enough to spread with a spatula but not melted. Spread the ice cream across almost the entire surface of the cake, leaving a small border bare at the sides. Carefully reroll the cake back into a spiral, wrap in plastic wrap and then aluminum foil. Freeze until ice cream is hardened. To serve, unwrap and slice the spiral crosswise into rounds with a serrated knife dipped in hot water.

WEIGHTS & MEASURES

COOKING MEASUREMENT EQUIVALENTS

16 tablespoons = 1 cup
2 cups = 1 pint
2 pints = 1 quart
3 teaspoons = 1 tablespoon
48 teaspoons = 1 cup

METRIC EQUIVALENTS
Capacity

1/5 teaspoon = 1 milliliter
1 teaspoon = 5 ml
1 tablespoon = 15 ml
1/5 cup = 50 ml
1 cup = 240 ml (about 1/4 liter)
2 cups (1 pint) = 470 ml
4 cups (1 quart) = .95 liter
4 quarts (1 gallon) = 3.8 liters

Weight

1 ounce = 30 grams
1 pound = 454 grams

OVEN TEMPERATURE GUIDE

	C	F
Warm	150	300
Moderately Warm	160	325
Medium	180	350
Moderately Hot	190	375
Hot	200-210	400-415
Broil	288	550

Other great regional cookbooks from Savory House Press

Sweet Southern: A Heritage of Beloved Desserts

"Anyone looking for a collection of traditional recipes – cakes, cobblers, pies – will want to check it out." –*The Tennesseean*. "The book's budget friendly price makes it the perfect item to keep on hand for last minute gifts." –*Houston Chronicle*. "This sweet little book offers the basic, best recipes for pies, pralines that helped make us what we are." –*Port Arthur News*. "Offers the South's favorite sweets!" –*Baton Rouge Advocate*.
88 pages. ISBN 1-892588-06-4. $5.95.

Salsa! Salsa! Salsa!

Crystal Walls' guide to making salsas for every occasion, to grace any cuisine. More than 70 varieties ensures you'll never run out of fresh ideas to serve up. "Hottest book on the shelf" – *Fort Worth Star-Telegram*. "This pocket sized book will surprise and delight you with its 75 creative and unique salsa recipes." –*Amazon* reader review.
88 pages. ISBN 1-892588-05-6. List $5.95.

Championship Chili

A guide to making chili, using recipes that swept top honors at the leading two national cook-offs. Includes a veteran competitor-judge's secrets on making a winning bowl of blessedness. "Best darn chili book in either direction of the Pecos" – *Big Bend Sentinel*. A portion of proceeds benefits the Big Bend Educational Foundation.
80 pages. ISBN 1-892588-03-X. $5.95.

Texas Chuckwagon Cuisine

"This small book packs a punch with tantalizing and intriguing recipes like splatter dabs, stolen chicken and drunken peach cobbler." – *The Monitor*, McAllen, Texas. It offers authentic cowboy trail cooking for the Dutch-oven enthusiast as well as for folks who want to make these traditional dishes in a modern kitchen using recipes from historic ranches.
80 pages. ISBN 978-1892588135. $5.95

Tex Mex 101

"From family favorites to gourmet creations, recipes from Texans who know" –*Sherman-Denison Herald-Democrat*. This handy guide makes genuine Texan-Mexican cuisine accessible to any kitchen. Includes fajitas, enchiladas, tres leches cake and Chef Dean Fearing's famous Turtle Mansion Tortilla Soup.
80 pages. ISBN 1-892588-02-1. $5.95.

Visit *www.savoryhousepress.com* to survey all of our scrumptious titles.